Praise For
The Rebirth of the Church

Bill Tuck has done it again! With wisdom and warmth, Bill offers a combination love letter and work order for reviving the Church. In a book filled with personal anecdotes and practical application, Bill offers encouragement, comfort and challenge for churches trying to find their way in a radically changing world. He writes with a passion for the church that is truly contagious. With hope and humor, he calls us to the true mission of the church: not survival of an institution but the salvation of the world. It is a delight to read, and also deserves careful study to absorb all that Bill offers from his diverse experiences in ministry.

David Moffett-Moore,
United Church of Christ minister
Author of *Wind and Whirlwind: Being a Pastor in a Storm of Change*

It is so refreshing to read a book from a minister who confesses in the preface that he has not given up on the church. In what I consider to be one of his best books, Bill Tuck offers a careful analysis of the many challenges facing the modern church and then offers a multitude of specific challenges of his own for its rebirth. From a lifetime of study, reflection, and ministry, Tuck addresses an amazing number of issues that trouble pastors and congregations alike. With the clarity, wisdom, and practicality that mark all his writing, he then offers concrete and specific perspectives and approaches to address these matters. Of the many books I have on my shelves about what is wrong with the church and how to fix it, this is by far the most comprehensive, the most biblical, the most theological, and the most doable. His conclusion, "My Dream for the Church", is not only an excellent summary of his book, but I also found it to be my dream as well. I believe you may also find it to be yours.

Ronald Higdon
Pastor Emeritus Broadway Baptist Church, Louisville, KY.
Author of *In Changing Times, Why Doesn't God Do Something?*

Pastors and parishioners alike will feel their hearts warmed by this extremely readable book from the pen of a favorite Christian author. Every chapter is replete with interesting thoughts about the church and entertaining stories and quotations that illustrate the thoughts. Don't miss this delightful read!

John Killinger
Former professor at Vanderbilt Divinity School
Pastor and author of many books, including *The Tender Shepherd and The Fundamentals of Preaching*

The struggles of the church in this time have been documented exhaustively, and extensive efforts have been made to assign blame or at least seek understanding, but not enough time has been invested in developing creative strategies to strengthen the church for the future. William Powell Tuck's new book *The Rebirth of the Church* addresses this need in profound and pragmatic ways.

Like all of Dr. Tuck's writing, *The Rebirth of the Church* reflects decades of pastoral ministry and biblical scholarship. These are the reflections of a faithful servant who loves the church as it is and can be, as well as the insights of a scholar who knows scripture and history. And unlike some attempts to stir numerical growth at all costs, Dr. Tuck argues for a renewed focus on authentic faith. Unlike those who target the forms of how we do church, Dr. Tuck focuses on the substance of the church, things like our love for Christ and each other, our calling to go beyond the walls of the church and share the Good News in all its fullness.

This is not to say that *The Rebirth of the Church* takes a naive approach to renewal and assumes that no changes in form are necessary. On the contrary, Dr. Tuck argues passionately for openness to change, only change that is grounded in spiritual purposes and genuine need.

In the end, this is a book of hope, authentic hope. It does not gloss over or minimize the realities of our time, but it does envision a hopeful future for the church based primarily on the goodness of God, and it offers a wide range of suggestions for how we can participate in this hopeful future. At one point, Dr. Tuck references Carlyle Marney's observation, "People say that the Church is always dying, but it never does." All who embrace this claim will find *The Rebirth of the Church* hopeful and helpful.

Chris Chapman
Senior Pastor, First Baptist Church, Raleigh, N. C.

"For everything there is a time and a season… a time to be born and a time to die" says Ecclesiastes. I would add there is also a time to be "reborn." The church of Jesus Christ, especially, needs a rebirth. This is notably true in the Northern Hemisphere where the church, in many places, looks like it is on its deathbed. In his latest book, *The Rebirth of the Church*, life-long pastor and scholar Bill Tuck thoughtfully and boldly challenges the church to rethink her mission in this skeptical age in which anything formally established, like the church, is viewed with suspicion. In these 14 essays, which were themes he preached on over the course of his pastoral career as a local church pastor, Tuck has crafted a much-needed narrative that is packed with insight from biblical, theological, and ethical perspectives that is uniquely refreshing in a time and season that is constantly shifting. He translates his insights into practical tools that provide a framework for clergy and lay renewal, reignited passion for sharing the gospel in unassuming and creative ways, and life again. For the church to live, she must be reborn, and Tuck reminds us that this is the time and season for her rebirth.

Jimmy Gentry
Senior Pastor, Garden Lakes Baptist Church, Rome, GA

William Powell Tuck, a native of Virginia, has served as a pastor in Virginia, Kentucky, North Carolina and Louisiana, and as a seminary professor, adjunct college professor and an intentional interim pastor. He is the author of 38 books including *The Journey to the Undiscovered Country: What's Beyond Death*, *Modern Shapers of Baptist Thought in America*, *The Church Under the Cross*, and *The Forgotten Beatitude: Worshiping Through Stewardship*. He was given an honorary Doctor of Divinity degree from the University of Richmond and in 1997 he received the "Pastor of the Year" award from the Academy of Parish Clergy. In 2016, he received the Wayne Oates Award from the Oates Institute in Louisville, Kentucky. He and his wife, Emily Campbell, are the parents of 2 children and 5 grandchildren and live in Midlothian Virginia.

Other Books by William Powell Tuck

Facing Grief and Death
The Struggle for Meaning (editor)
Knowing God: Religious Knowledge in the Theology of John Baillie
Our Baptist Tradition
Ministry: An Ecumenical Challenge (editor)
Getting Past the Pain
A Glorious Vision
The Bible as Our Guide for Spiritual Growth (editor)
Authentic Evangelism
The Lord's Prayer Today
The Way for All Seasons
Through the Eyes of a Child
Christmas Is for the Young…Whatever Their Age
Love as a Way of Living
The Compelling Faces of Jesus
The Left Behind Fantasy
The Ten Commandments: Their Meaning Today
Facing Life's Ups and Downs
The Church in Today's World
The Church Under the Cross
Modern Shapers of Baptist Thought in America
The Journey to the Undiscovered Country: What's Beyond Death?
A Pastor Preaching: Toward a Theology of the Proclaimed Word
The Pulpit Ministry of the Pastors of River Road Church, Baptist (editor)
The Last Words from the Cross
Lord, I Keep Getting a Busy Signal: Reaching for a Better Spiritual Connection
Overcoming Sermon Block: The Preacher's Workshop
A Revolutionary Gospel: Salvation in the Theology of Walter Rauschenbusch
Holidays, Holy Days, and Special Days
A Positive Word for Christian Lamenting: Funeral Homilies
The Forgotten Beatitude: Worshipping through Stewardship
Star Thrower: A Pastor's Handbook
A Pastoral Prophet: Sermons and Prayers of Wayne E. Oates (editor)

The Abiding Presence: Communion Meditations
Which Voice Will You Follow?
The Difficult Sayings of Jesus
Beginning and Ending a Pastorate
Conversations with My Grandchildren about God, Religion, and Life

The Rebirth of the Church

Responding to the Call to Christian Discipleship

William Powell Tuck

Energion Publications
Gonzalez, Florida
2020

Copyright © 2020, William Powell Tuck

Unless otherwise noted, Scripture quotations are from Revised Standard Version of the Bible, copyright © 1946, 1952, and 1971 National Council of the Churches of Christ in the United States of America. Used by permission. All rights reserved worldwide.

Scripture quotations marked Moffatt are from the James Moffatt, A New Translation of the Bible, Containing the Old and New Testaments. New York: Doran, 1926. Revised edition, New York and London: Harper and Brothers, 1935. Reprinted, Grand Rapids: Kregel, 1995.

Scripture quotations marked TEV are from the Good News Translation in Today's English Version-Second Edition. Copyright © 1992 by American Bible Society. Used by Permission.

Scripture Quotations marked Phil or Phillips are from The New Testament in Modern English, Copyright © 1958 by J. B. Phillips.

Scripture quotations marked NEB are taken from the New English Bible, copyright © Cambridge University Press and Oxford University Press 1961, 1970. All rights reserved.

Some Scripture quotations are the author's own translation.

ISBN: 978-1-63199-509-5
eISBN: 978-1-63199-514-9

Energion Publications
PO Box 841
Gonzalez, FL 32560

http://www.energionpubs.com
pubs@energion.com

With appreciation to
Bluefield College
where they encouraged me
and helped equip me educationally
as I began my preparation to serve as a minister

Table of Contents

Preface vii

1	Let God Kindle a Fire Within	1
2	On Building the Church	15
3	The Challenge of Change	27
4	In the Power of the Spirit	41
5	The Task of the Church Today	49
6	The Church Nobody Knows	61
7	The Rebirth of the Church	73
8	Why Go To Church?	85
9	The Ministry of the Church	99
10	Addressing the Gospel to Young Adults: Is God Over Thirty?	111
11	The Gospel's Challenge to Young People: An Open Letter to Bill as He Leaves for College	121
12	Going Home Again	133
13	Like a Mighty Army	145
14	My Dream For The Church: A Summary	157

Preface

The Christian Church is in a time of transition, evolving, transformation, re-evaluation, and some say even dying. Some churches have indeed died, and their buildings have now been transformed into restaurants, museums, art galleries, motels, schools, parking lots, or just torn down. I have served as an interim pastor in several churches that could seat five hundred or more in their sanctuary and that now struggle to have fifty persons present for worship in the same building. What is the cause of this decline in church attendance today? Countless reasons are given. For some, it may be a part of their general distrust of all institutions like the government, the news media, etc. Many persons are just not interested in going to worship on Sunday. They had rather use the time to relax, participate in recreation, visit family or friends, shop, sleep late, travel, watch television, go to the mountains or beach, or dozens of other reasons could fill the page. The "nones" and many of the millennials seem little concerned about institutional religion. They may claim to be spiritual but not religious, certainly in the sense of attending a church service on Sunday morning. In a 2018 survey, the number of "nones," those who don't affiliate with any specific faith tradition, now are tied with Catholics and evangelicals in the largest religious groupings in our country.[1] Some have vacated the church pews because of what they call the "two-faced" version of the Christian faith among many church goers and the moral contradictions in their everyday living. Another reason for others is the attitude some say that the church has toward the LGBT persons, the role of women in the church and society, and the sexual immorality of many of the religious

---

1 "Number of nones equals evangelicals, Catholic," *Christian Century* (April 24, 2019), 17.

leaders, priests and ministers, in the church today. Referring to the early Church's anointing at Pentecost, Barrie Shepherd raises the question of what has happened to that "bright descending light" in this question:

> But that bright descending fire
> that melted hearts to kindness sent them
> out across all gulfs to spend themselves for
> others' sakes, what put it out? Or why has it
> flamed fainter, ever fainter with the years?
> Is there a sacred oil can yet rekindle such a spark?
> Or are we doomed to batter one another with
> the truth through the encroaching dark? [2]

This book is one minister's efforts to challenge the institutional church to finds ways to ignite that Pentecostal flame again, to discover how the Church can be "re-born" again, to reach out to the non-churched today, also to re-engage its own church members to take seriously the challenge of sharing the good news of the Gospel with others. Christians must be rekindled in their enthusiasm for sharing the Gospel and restore their commitment to following the Great Commission of our Lord. As someone has said, "The church is always one generation away from extinction." Is this going to be that generation? If church members will take seriously their commitment to follow Christ, then once again the church may be able to move "like a mighty army." This may cause the church to face many changes in structure, organization, leadership roles, the status of professional ministers, ways and times of worship, places to meet, breaking of denominational barriers, the ethical standards of its ministers, and even re-evaluating some of its doctrines.

Will the Church have the will and courage to face this challenge? If the Church is going to survive, it must respond to its call to Christian discipleship. Brian McLaren's recent book, *The Great Spiritual Migration*, is a summons for the church to move away

---

2   J. Barrie Shepherd, *Between Mirage and Miracle* (Eugene, Oregon: WIPF & Stock, 2012), 37.

from a status-quo, dogmatic, rigidly established system of belief, and narrow religion to one that is an open and daring spiritual journey that focuses not so much on one's own personal religion but one's neighbor and the world itself.[3] McLaren has presented, in my opinion, a summons that beckons to all Christians who take seriously, or should take seriously, the call to be a disciple of Christ. I affirm his challenge.

In most of the chapters in this book, I have been open and upfront in my challenge for the Church to respond to the summons from Christ to discipleship. I reach back to the foundation of the Church Christ established, and seek to guide us forward from our initial commitment to Christ into our present walk with him in service and love. I do not believe that one can be an authentic believer in Christ and not worship, share the Good News with others, support persons in need, and strive to grow in our faith. In several of the chapters, like "Is God Over Thirty?" "An Open Letter to Bill as He Leaves for College," and "Going Home Again," I invite the reader to "overhear" the message, to use Fred Craddock's phrase. Sometimes the indirect approach may be more effective than a direct one. But I have not hesitated to be very direct in my summons for the Church to rise and respond to Christ's call to a servant and pilgrim discipleship. I have not given up on the Church. I believe Christ is still working in the hearts and minds of persons to follow him into the unknown, challenging future with the message of Christ's love and redemption. I hope to see the Church enlivened and rekindled to proclaim the Good News and live out the servant ministry Christ has call us to undertake. I commit my life to that end. I extend again my words of appreciation to my fellow minister and friend, Rand Forder, for reading this manuscript in its early stages.

---

3   Brian D. McLaren, *The Great Spiritual Migration* (New York: Convergent Books, 2016).

I

Let God Kindle a Fire Within

One of the haunting memories from my childhood, and one which has been reinforced repeatedly by my parents retelling the episode, was an experience I had as a small child. One day I walked into the woods near where we lived. I had taken a box of matches with me which I had seen lying on the stove. I had decided to build a fire like the ones I had seen other people start. I gathered some sticks and leaves and placed them in a small pile. Then I took a match from the box, struck it, and put its flame against the leaves. Instantly the leaves began to burn, and soon the twigs burst into flames. They began to burn and burn and burn. And soon the whole woods was on fire!

At that point, I did what any small child would do. I ran for home. I could hear the sirens of the fire truck off in the distance. Someone had seen the fire and called the fire department. I ran up the steps of our house and went upstairs into our attic. I sat down in a rocking chair there and began to rock back and forth. My mother did not have to ask me: "Who started that fire?" She knew who had done it. The fact that I went rushing from the fire up to the attic and did not bother to go see the fire engines was very revealing to her. She said that this was one of the few lessons from which I did not have to have some other reinforcements to enable me to remember them. Later as I became older, I learned through Boy Scouts how to build fires properly in the woods.

We have all had some experiences with fire. Some of you may have been the victims of a fire in your home. A hotel near the church I was pastoring in another city, burned to the ground. While I was away at college, I heard that a large part of the downtown section of my hometown burned down. We have seen pictures on T.V. of the walls of flames that have consumed so much of our national forests and a whole town in California. As a congregation, St. Matthews Baptist Church, where I served as pastor, experienced the loss of its church buildings by fire before I began my ministry with them. We all know something about fire. Images and memories of it fill our minds.

FIRE AS A POWERFUL SYMBOL

In the Bible, fire is used as a powerful symbol. In the Old Testament Moses encounters God in the flames of a burning bush which is not consumed. God led the children of Israel at night with a pillar of fire. The children of Israel on Mt. Sinai worshiped God. Some scholars believe that Sinai was a volcano or maybe some thunderstorms were constantly at its top. But the Sinai concept of God as fire had a tremendous impact on the children of Israel and their understanding of God. Elijah departed this life in a chariot of fire. John the Baptist said that "there was one who was coming after him who will baptize with water and with fire." Jesus said to His disciples, "I have seeded you with fire." In the Book of Revelation, the writer tells us that the appearance of the Christ will be with "eyes like flames of fire" (Revelation 1:14).

Jesus Christ was himself the torch that ignited the flame that came into the world. In Luke 12: 49, we capture an insight into the very heart of Christ himself. He seems to be saying that he has feelings of reluctance in what he must do, but he also discloses a sense of impatience. He cries: "Oh, I would that the fire had already come, that it was already kindled." In Christ we recognize that the fire is not truly kindled until his death comes. Jesus knew the baptism that awaited him--the baptism of fire--was suffering, crucifixion, and death. He did not go toward that crisis enthusiastically, but reluctantly and, yet he knew that through that crisis experience would come the refiner's fire of judgement. Jesus knew the opposition and persecution which his gospel would create.

But how startling the claim seems to sound from Christ. "I, a Galilean peasant, will set a fire on the earth that will burn with a raging fury." But he did! This same Christ brought the fire of heaven down to earth in the incarnation of his spirit. This very Christ, when his body was broken, set loose a fire that has raged down through the centuries to bring men and women to Christ. He is literally the torch that transforms lives. His death was the baptism which launched his kingdom.

FIRE AS METAPHOR FOR JUDGMENT

Think with me about some of the metaphors for fire which we find within the Scriptures. Fire is sometimes used as a metaphor for the judgment of God. Fire in the Scriptures is often symbolic of the consuming, terrible wrath, and judgment of God. The Book of Hebrews, the twelfth chapter and the twentieth verse, tells us that God is a consuming fire. In our day and age, we spend a great deal of time, which is very important to do, talking about God as a God of love. But I am convinced that sometimes our understanding of the love of God has made God's love like mush. There is no depth or substance to it. There is no understanding of the disciplined side of love which is judgment. Any parent who really loves his or her child will give them a sense of disciplined love. They will not offer to them the freedom to be and do anything they might want. We have to understand that there is responsibility which goes with one's actions. Love from God's perspective carries judgment with it. Sometimes, as we encounter the power of his holiness, our sinfulness does stand in judgment and needs to be transformed and changed.

FIRE AS PURIFYING

Fire in God's judgment is seen as purifying. When your spirit and mine encounter the grace and love of God. God doesn't say to us: "Oh, it's o.k. It doesn't make any difference what you do or what you say." God comes and says to us: "Be holy as I am holy."

We are challenged to seek to be like God. Our lives are encountered by is spirit, and we are lifted up to be purified so that we may be more like he is.

When ore is placed in fire, impurities rise scum-like to the top and are ladled off. Ore is purified by the process of burning. As we come into the burning presence of God and stand in his judging grace, we experience the power of redemption which is transforming and purifying. God then points us in a new direction because we have become new creations.

Fire as Revealing

But fire is also revealing. I love to watch wood when I throw it into the fire. You can tell something about what kinds of oils, acids, and other ingredients are in the wood by the way it burns. Elm burns very slowly because it is damp. Green sycamore is like a rock and is almost impossible to burn. Balsam or hemlock, when placed in the fire, explodes sending sparks in every direction as though they want to take somebody with them in their demise. White paper birch sends up a yellow flame. Apple wood sends up a multi-colored flame. Hickory, the hardest wood of all, sends forth a very hot flame. The flames reveal the ingredients of the wood in their process of burning.

The burning of wood reveals something of its inner nature. I have walked with some persons through their fires of difficulties, pain, suffering, and turmoil. I have seen revealed in the lives of so many within this congregation inner strength, faith, and courage. In the times of testing these people have revealed a deep abiding faith. When our church experienced its great ordeal by fire, many of you were present then, and you have shown a strong inner fortitude, a deep faith, and continued faithfulness in your support of this congregation. Fire reveals something of our inner nature.

FIRE PROVIDING LIGHT

Fire sometimes provides light. In England, for example, when persons refer to a flashlight, they call it a torch. Their "torch" throws a light on a path so one can walk in its light. Fire is a source of light and guidance for direction in our lives. Christ becomes the supreme fire of light. From his presence we find light to walk in the world.

CHRIST AS A DISTURBING FIRE

In the metaphor that Jesus used about fire in Luke 12: 49, it is depicted as a disturbing force. The torch of Christ in the world comes as a disturbing force, as fire often is. It comes with consuming power. It comes demanding loyalty to him. He says, "I am the way." You must realize, he says, that if you commit your life to me, it is a narrow way. It may cause, Jesus says, separation from families and friends. Sometimes it may cause misunderstandings and rejection, because the Christ who comes as a disturbing force in our lives, challenges us to follow in His way and to be like Him.

When I was a summer missionary in Hawaii, while I was a student in college, a young man, who was Japanese by birth, committed his life to Jesus Christ and accepted Him as Lord. When he made this decision, he was no longer considered a part of his family because of his commitment to Jesus Christ as Lord. It was costly and disturbing to him. Do we have this kind of commitment today?

In one of his books, Karl Barth wrote powerfully about the spirit of Christ as fire in the world. He observed: "Oh yes there is much *smoke* upon the earth, smoke of fervid, urgent love for God and man; smoke of quiet, sincere faith; smoke of anxious, unshakable hope; smoke of profound, progressive ideas, ideas so exhausted that they reach that beyond which we cannot think; smoke of noble, courageous zeal for the good; smoke of universal movements for the betterment and re-creation of temporal circumstances. Who would dare to ignore this rising smoke? ... Where there is smoke there surely is a glow, always and always the glow that Jesus has started. But smoke is not fire, even if there is ever so much smoke."[4] There is a great deal of smoke today. But I sometimes wonder where is the fiery zeal that Christ has called us to have. It is not always very evident.

When I was a graduate student at Emory University in Atlanta, Georgia, I had an opportunity to preach several times in a church not too far from campus. The church was in a declining neighborhood. The church building was large and probably seated about 800 people. But on Sunday morning when they met to worship, they would have only about fifty people gathered there. It was a difficult church to try to preach in, because they had pulled so much into themselves and took no interest in their community around them. Their chief thought was simply to preserve their building and church as it was at that particular moment. The church was dead because they had no desire to be any more than they were. They were content and had no desire to change or grow.

One Sunday while I was preaching there, the fire alarm went off in the church building. Someone went immediately to see if there was a fire. Finally, someone came back and told us that there was no fire. It was only a false alarm. But I started thinking. I wondered if God's spirit sought to break into the lives of those people, if they would be as disturbed as they had been when the fire alarm went off that day. For most of us, if God's spirit really touched us in a service of worship, we would be as surprised as though a fire alarm had gone off. It would be unexpected, and in no way would we have sought it. We come repeatedly to worship without expectation or looking for the spirit of God to come into our lives. But there was no fire in that church in any way!

Several years ago, St. Matthews Baptist Church's building burned down. However, the church didn't burn down. Only the buildings burned down. A church needs to be on fire. The people in the building need to have a vital sense of having been touched

---

[4] Karl Barth and Eduard Thurneysen, *Come Holy Spirit* (Grand Rapids: William B. Eerdmans, Co., 1978), 112-113

The Rebirth of the Church

by the powerful presence of God. God's presence may come into our lives to disturb us and drive us into action.

FIRE AS TRANSFORMING

Fire comes as a transforming element. When we put coal, wood, gas, or oil into fire, it becomes heat, energy, or light. It is transmuted. It goes from what it was to what it can be, and it takes on a newness. Christ has come into our lives to transform us, to give us a newness, to give us new direction, to make us other than we have been. He points us to be what God created us to be.

In 1624 the French philosopher Pascal had an experience with Christ which he said was so overwhelming, radiant, and powerful that there was only one word that could describe it. He wrote his experience down and pinned it to the inside of his coat. He said that word was "Fire." God had come into his life in such a moving way that he had been transformed.

Nels F. S. Ferre' quoted a prayer a number of years ago that expressed his experience with God:

> Come as the fire and burn.
> Come as the wind and cleanse.
> Come as light and reveal.
> Convict, convert, consecrate.
> Until we are wholly thine.[5]

God comes into our lives to transform us and bring us in harmony with his spirit. God moves within us to stimulate us to be his people in the world to share his grace with others.

CHRIST AS THE FIERY TORCH

Jesus Christ is the fiery torch. He lifts his torch to show us the way to life. We are reminded that fire is also a symbol of life. We are absolutely dependent on the sun for light and life here. Without the flaming ball of the sun, we would not have light or

---

5   Nels F. S. Ferre', quoted in Elton Trueblood, *The Incendiary Fellowship* (New York: Harper & Row, 1967), 108-109

heat. We acknowledge that fire and heat are essential for life. Fire is a symbol for life. Christ is the flame of real life. He is the one who gives illumination. He is the one who brings us life. He is the one who has brought "the life" into the world to ignite it with real living. He, when He is lifted up, gives us light to guide our walk so that we can see how to live as redeemed persons.

Fire as Warmth

Fire is also a metaphor for warmth. I hope as a congregation we will extend to others something of the personal warmth of the experience we have in Jesus Christ. Though we may be a large congregation, we should never forget that God works primarily through persons. God is concerned not with masses of people but with individuals, and he reaches out to you and to me with the warmth of His presence to love us and to care for us personally.

I remember an experience I had in graduate school with a noted professor. He had written a dozen books or more and was known internationally for his great scholarship. I recall one day taking an assigned paper by his office to give it to him. I knocked on the door. He came to the door and opened it just wide enough to see me and said, "Yes," I said, "Dr. So and So, I have the paper you asked us to turn in." He opened the door just far enough to receive the paper and said, "Thank you," and closed the door. Now I learned, not just through that experience, but through the experience I had with him in class, that he was mostly concerned with ideas. He was basically interested in the abstract and his own or other's understanding of philosophy. He was not interested in us as persons and only interested in us as students as we helped in his research and formulation of his own ideas.

I hope that our church will never give an image to people that we, who claim to have experienced the power and warmth of God's presence, are only interested in masses or large numbers of people but are not interested in individual persons. I think we have missed the essence of the gospel itself and the spirit of Christ when we do not care for individuals and love them and minister to them.

FIRE AS ENCOURAGING

Fire has always been an encouragement to me. I love a fire in the fireplace. When I used to camp a lot, there was nothing friendlier or more encouraging than to have the warmth of a fire at night or early morning on a camping scene. Fire is a sign of encouragement, and we all need encouraging. Who among us does not have low moments? There are times when somebody else needs to lift us up and to say the right word. I hope, as a congregation which has been tested by fire, difficult experiences, and having been displaced, that now we shall be better people because of what we have been through. I hope that we shall be more encouraging to others and more caring because of what we have learned in our trial by fire.

John Killinger tells of a regionalist writer in Maine whose name was Sarah Ome Jewett. She wrote once about an old spinster named Miss Tempey. In her account, she described the watchers who had come to "watch" on the night before the burial service for Miss Tempey. Two elderly women were talking about the spinster and they began to reminisce about the marvelous quince jelly that she used to make. They agreed that it was the best jelly they had ever eaten. Then they began to wonder about the thorny, half-dead, old quince tree from which she got the fruit for her jelly. They confessed they didn't know how she did it, but she always seemed to be able to encourage that old tree to bear one more year. She always seemed to be able to encourage it to give one more crop.

We need more encouragers. We need those who will say the right word at the right moment, those who will give an embrace at the right occasion. We need more people who will show concern to us at the needed time. We all need to have a strong sense of the warmth of encouragement.

Fire as Inspiration

But fire is also a symbol for inspiration. We speak of persons being "on fire." They are filled with the fires of enthusiasm. The "tongues of fire" recorded in the Book of Acts came upon the disciples and filled them with inspiration and enthusiasm to go preach and serve in the name of Christ.

Those who have caught something of the illumination of Christ will have the fire and zeal of his spirit filling their lives. There is nothing worse than trying to warm up frozen spirits. It's much easier, I think, to try to cool a volcano than it is to try to heat up an iceberg. Sometimes I would rather have people who are overly enthusiastic than those who don't have any enthusiasm. Jesus Christ has come to ignite us with the zeal of His spirit. He has come to set us aflame as his people in the world to work and serve in his name. We are to be, to use Elton Trueblood's phrase, "The Incendiary Fellowship." In his rousing hymn, Trueblood has challenged us to be aglow with God's spirit.

> Thou, whose purpose is to kindle:
> Now ignite us with Thy fire;
> While the earth awaits Thy burning.
> With Thy passion inspire.
> Overcome our sinful calmness,
> Rouse us with redemptive shame;
> Baptize with Thy fiery Spirit.
> Crown our lives with tongues of flame.[6]

Ignited by the Flame of Christ

Jerome Ellison, in a book entitled *Report to the Creator*, tells about an experience he had as a youth in his home church. While he was at worship, he had an experience with the power of God's spirit that touched his life. He said he became so excited that he could hardly wait for the benediction to discuss his feelings with his parents and some other adults and to tell them about the ex-

---

6   Trueblood, *Ibid*, 11

The Rebirth of the Church

citement that had been created in his spirit by God. But everybody was busy talking about other matters, and nobody had time for him. Finally, someone did notice him but only remarked that he looked pale. Another said that maybe church was too much for him and laughed. He was deeply crushed and concluded that all adults were hypocrites. This experience led him to years of religious indifference and doubt. Years later, after much study and thought, he returned to church and said the amazing thing was that as an adult God reached down and touched him again in that worship service and his experience was ignited again by the presence of God. But he said, "Now I was an adult, I would not remain silent. Whenever there was an opportunity I spoke shouting, "Look who is here!"[7] Look who is here in this place of worship and many of you have not seen him. He is come that we might experience the power of his presence. Look he is here!

Walter Russell Bowie wrote a book several years ago entitled *Men of Fire,* which today would have to be retitled *Men and Women of Fire.* In his book, Bowie traced twenty-six exciting biographies of torchbearers of the Gospel from biblical days to the present. He writes about Jesus' statement: "1 have come to cast fire upon the earth." "So, Jesus said to his disciples; and the fire indeed was kindled. It would be a fire of affliction in which their courage would be tested, as gold in the furnace is tried, a fire on the altar of sacrifice where fear and selfishness could be burned away. It would also be like the light of a lamp to illuminate their minds and consciences; and a flame within their hearts to burn there as an unquenchable devotion."[8]

Jesus Christ comes into our lives. His presence comes as a flame to make us different. The flame of his presence refines us, cleanses us, directs us, empowers us, and inspires us. It comes and touches us in such a way with the power of is grace and love that other people can see that the torch of His experience has ignited us.

---

7   Jerome Ellison, *Report to the Creator* (New York: Harper & Bros., 1955), 201, 205.
8   Walter Russell Bowie, *Men of Fire* (New York: Harper & Bros., 1961), ix.

Harry Emerson Fosdick tells about a young man whom he was counseling who was a borderline alcoholic. He worked with that young man for months before he was able to control his drive. When this young man came to Fosdick he was not a believer, but when he left Fosdick after his last counseling session he said: "If you ever find anyone who doesn't believe in God, send him to me. I know."[9] He was living proof that God can make a difference in a person's life.

Your life and my life, when the experience and power of God have ignited it, should be radically different. I hope that the enthusiasm and the power of God's spirit will permeate your life and mine. I pray that we will be excited about God's presence in our lives. I hope that you and I will be ignited by God's flame and excited about our church as the place for us where God is seeking to work in our community.

Jesus said, "I have come to cast fire on the earth." If you and I are really going to minister and be the kind of church that Christ wants us to be, there has to be that fiery glow within us that comes from the presence of a living Lord who makes all things new within us.

One evening Emily and I were walking down the main street in Edinburgh, Scotland. As darkness began to fall on the city, I remembered a story I had heard years ago. This story was about a stranger who came to Edinburgh around the turn of the century before the city had electric lights and the street lamps were lit with gas. The visitor to the city was standing on the balcony of his hotel when he saw the lamplighter approach. The lamplighter reached up to the lamp with his torch and thrust it into the gas light. The lamp exploded into a flame. The visitor watched the lamplighter as he continued to walk down the street and stop and set his torch to touch another light, and it began to glow. He seemed to be punching holes in the darkness. He watched the lamplighter until he finally disappeared. He could see the lights bursting into flames

---

9   Lionel G. Crocker (ed), *Harry Emerson Fosdick's Art of Preaching: An Anthology* (Springfield: Charles C. Thomas Publishers, 1971), 52.

here and then there. Another lamp burst into flames, and then another, then another, and another, and another.

When you and I leave the church when we worship, we ought to go into the world to let our lives be flames of light for Christ. Jesus said, "I have come to cast fire upon the earth, and I wish it were already kindled." Through the baptism of his death and sacrifice, he has kindled that fire. You and I have responded. Let that glow of his love so radiate from your life that in all that you do others will see and be drawn to Christ and experience his love and grace.

2

ON BUILDING THE CHURCH

The late Wallace Hamilton, who for many years was the pastor of the Community Church in Pasadena, Florida, was arriving late for an annual conference where he was scheduled to preach. As he came up the steps, he saw a group of small boys playing on the front steps of the church. They paused in their playing and were peering into the open windows where the sound of music was coming. As he placed his hand on the church door to open it and go in, one of the young boys turned and said to him: "Hey mister, what's going on in there?" That question needs to be heard by the Church today. What goes on in here? What goes on in the Church? What really is the Church? What is going on in it?

That is the question people have been asking down through the centuries. What is happening in Church? Some have come back rather quickly and forcefully and answered: "Not much!" The tribe of "nones"- non-attenders- has risen drastically. Some have said the last days of the Church are here. Books and speeches have been written about *The Noise of Solemn Assembly, The Empty Pulpit, The Comfortable Pew, The Last Days of the Church, Demise of the Church, The Death of the American Church,* and *The Dying Church.* The *Newsweek* magazine had a cover several years ago with the inscription: "Forget the Church. Follow Jesus." Some voices say that the Church is coming close to its demise. Its end is near. But I think Carlyle Marney is correct when he observed that "people say that the Church is always dying, but it never does." Most of the hammers of criticism that have been beaten against the Church have been worn out eventually on the anvil of the Church itself. The Church continues to endure.

Biblical Images of the Church

When we turn to the New Testament, we find some **interesting figures for the Church.** Images of all kind abound. The Church is depicted as the Bride of Christ, the Body of Christ, the Household of Faith, the Family of Jehovah, the Seat and Shrine of the Eternal, the New Israel, the New Covenant, the Realm of Redemption, salt, light, leaven, and the vine. But I suppose Paul's favorite metaphor is the Temple or the building as seen in Ephesians 2: 19-22. Jesus himself said, "I will build my Church." When congregations have a building in the process of being constructed, they need to remember that the constructed building will house the church. A part of what we must always keep before us and in proper focus is that the building is never the Church. It houses the Church. The building has a function to carry on the ministry of the Church which is being built. We are the building. The Church, when it is properly constructed, is a living structure.

The Foundation of the Church

Paul, in the second chapter of the Letter to the Ephesians, writes about building the Church of Christ. The apostles and the New Testament prophets, which Paul mentions here, **are the foundation of the Church.** Jesus Christ himself is the **chief cornerstone** in the foundation. Some scholars believe that the foundation stone in ancient buildings was a huge stone that may have been seven feet in its scope. Others are not convinced that the stone is in its foundation but is instead the gem stone, which is the stone set in the archway of the building. That stone is called the foundation stone and kept the whole structure fitted together so it could not fall apart. Whether the emphasis is on the foundation or on the archway, it is basically the same: Christ is the foundation stone which holds the Church together.

The Rebirth of the Church

THE BASIC STONES IN THE CHURCH'S FOUNDATION

As we reflect on the Church, we need to understand what some of the **basic stones are within the church's foundation.** When these stones are incorporated in the foundation, they will enable us to build a structure worthy of being called the Church of Christ. A church building under construction is important, but even more important is the building of the people. We the people constitute the Church, and the building houses the Church, so we can be Christ's people in the world.

THE FOUNDATION OF PERSONAL COMMITMENT

Paul wrote about the necessity of the **foundation of the apostles and the prophets. You and I are also a part of that kind of foundation.** We are a part of the continuing building of the Church by our own sense of commitment as new disciples to the Christ as the early disciples were by their initial commitment to him. One of the cardinal stones in the foundation of the Church is the **personal experience** of individual people who have committed their lives to Jesus Christ. Our faith is supposed to be very personal, just as the early disciples had a very personal experience with Christ. Now, granted we cannot go back and walk with the living Christ along the shores of Galilee, but Jesus Christ needs to be a real presence for us. Our experience should be so real that we sense the power of his presence that changes and transforms us. Sometimes that is a part of the problem with the Church today. This essential stone in the foundation is often lacking. The Church is not always made up of people who have committed their lives to Christ and have had a genuine personal experience with Christ. Press the pause button on that thought for a moment.

I heard about a young girl who went to visit a relative of hers who lived in the country. One night while she was visiting her aunt she noticed that her aunt was putting cold cream on her face before she went to bed. The small girl turned and asked: "Auntie, what are you doing?" She said, "Why, I'm making myself beautiful." In a few moments her aunt began to remove the cream. The small girl looked at her aunt and said: "It didn't work, did it?"

Press the pause button again now. Note, there are some folks who are looking at the Church and saying to it: "It didn't work, did it?" We claim that we are a people who have experienced the vitality of a living Christ, and they are saying to us: "It didn't work, did it?" They often do not see evidence of Christ in the lives of those who claim that they belong to the Church. Our relationship to Christ is not by proxy, but it is personal. It is not a second-hand experience but a first-hand one. It is not a hearsay experience but an immediate one. It is not something merely passed on to us by tradition. The Church began with a great claim: "I know whom I have believed" (2Timothy 1:12). In the small Epistle of John, the writer says: "That which we have seen with our eyes, that which we have heard with our ears, that which we have handled with our hands, we declare unto you" (1 John 1:1). It is a very personal experience with a living Christ. Vitality in the Church does not come by proxy, or by someone living on another's experience. A vital Church is built on individuals who have had their own dynamic relationship with the Lord of the Church.

Pastors and professors are often having tours. So, I thought of a tour group that I could organize. I might call it "Tuck's Back to God Movement." We might see if we could go back to places where people say they have experienced God. We could go back and try to find the place where Abraham was willing to go searching for a city that was without foundation. We would see if we could find the place where Jacob experienced the angels ascending and descending a ladder before God. We would see if we could find the remains of the bush that was burning where Moses had an experience with God. We would see if we could discover the ruins of the temple where Isaiah saw God high and lifted up. We would see if we could find the footprints in the sand where the disciples followed Jesus and left their nets and went to become fishers of men. Or we could see if we could find the place on the Damascus Road where Paul had his blinding experience with Christ. We would move on

The Rebirth of the Church 19

down through history and see if we could find the garden spot where Augustine heard the voice that said, "take up and read," and he himself was converted. Or we would climb the stairs in Rome where Luther searched to find the Spirit of God. Or we could go to Aldersgate where Wesley's heart was strangely warmed.

But there are several problems with that kind of a tour. For one thing, you probably cannot find those spots. But the biggest problem with it is that it is always focused in the past. We seem to think that we must go back someplace and find out what God did for somebody back there in the past. But the angel said to those who came to the tomb searching for Jesus, "You seek Jesus of Nazareth, but he is not here, he has gone before you." Christ is always going before his Church and seeks to draw us into the future. He is not content with what we have been or where we have been. We are built on that foundation, and we are aware that Jesus Christ is indeed the central foundation. Where Christ is, there is his Church. Where Christ is absent, his Church is not there, no matter what kind of building we may have. Churches need to construct a building in which the living Christ is Lord. In fact, a part of what Paul is saying in this passage is that the loving God wants to be in a living temple. Paul changes the metaphor about the stones and pictures the stones as living. The Church is not just brick and mortar, but it is made up of living people.

Robert Raines was putting his young son to bed once when the boy looked up at him and said: "Daddy, tell me again what does Maundy Thursday mean?" In their Church tradition, they were celebrating a special service on the Thursday before Easter. Dr. Raines told him that Maundy Thursday was the night that Jesus had his last meal with his disciples. They ate together, and Jesus talked to them about what that meal symbolized. He left the upper room and later was crucified on Good Friday, and then he was raised from the dead by God. We celebrate Easter because of the great event of the resurrection of Christ. Then the young son looked at his father and asked: "Daddy, will Easter ever happen to me?"

Isn't the Church supposed to be composed of those who claim that we have experienced Easter? We worship a living Christ who is Lord of the Church. A strong sense of a vital, personal experience with Jesus Christ is the foundation of the Church, if it is to be authentic Church.

The Foundation of Worship

You will also notice that Paul writes about the Church **being knit together as a holy temple.** The Temple is a place where people focus on worship. I frankly do not know how people live who do not worship. I spend a lot of my time dealing with religious matters and reading religious books. But I know that there is an absolute necessity for worship in my life. Worship is not something I can choose to do or not do. It is not a decision I make like whether I will go swimming or go to the mountains or to a lake or beach. Worship, according to the biblical understanding of it, is something a Christian does. It is not debatable. A Christian worships, if he or she really does care about God. Worship is essential to the vitality of an individual and to the vitality of a church.

Let me tell you a parable. One day Mr. or Ms. Spider walked out on a limb. He or she dropped a silver thread down from that limb and began to spin a beautiful web across a rushing stream that lay beneath it. Now Mr. or Ms. Spider sat on this delightful web and enjoyed it for some time capturing whatever came along for lunch, supper, or other occasions. Time went by and there was a great sense of satisfaction and delight in Mr. or Ms. Spider. But, then, one day the spider looked up at the silver thread which attached it to the limb, and asked: "What is that for? I don't need that." With one sweep, it was severed and the whole web went crashing into the stream below. And the spider was swept away.

I am astounded at how often we live like that. We think we can live without the vital cord that relates us to the God of the universe. So, we sever it, and we go our way without any kind of focus on God. Then we wonder why our life seems to be caught in

The Rebirth of the Church

the rapids of destructive elements which toss us in all directions. Worship sustains us; without it we die spiritually. To be meaningful, worship is not an occasional affair, but is practiced day after day, week after week, and year after year.

The Bible depicts many persons falling prostrate before God in worship and declaring: "Holy, holy is his name." They freely acknowledge the mystery, power, and the awesome nature of the God of the universe. I worship for many reasons. I worship out of *a sense of thanksgiving*. I recall the time when my wife came back from surgery, and we received word that everything was fine. A sense of thanksgiving came to my lips. When my children were born, I remember going in their room and examining them and, then, expressing my sense of thanksgiving to God. I can still envision standing as a young man in the mountains of Virginia on an early summer morning and watching the sun rise above the lake as it sent its silhouette against the water and expressing a sense of thanksgiving to the Creator – God.

I also worship out of *a sense of need*. I acknowledge my own vulnerability. I acknowledge that I am not sufficient in and of myself and that I am not self-made. I need the great God of the universe, and I need the fellowship of the community of faith. I acknowledge my need as you also have a need. Some of you have moved to this community full of strangers, and there is a need. Some of you look across the table at an empty chair, and there is a need for worship. Some of you are struggling with problems with your family, with your husband or wife, your children, or aged parents, and there is a need in your life. There are those present who have financial problems. Many here are struggling with all kinds of dilemmas and difficulties and need the strength and power that comes from a source beyond ourselves. We have to acknowledge that we are not sufficient for all of this. I worship because of my own vulnerability. One accident in the bathtub, or one drunken driver who has lost control of his automobile, can change my whole life in an instant.

Worship becomes for us *an oasis in time*. We set apart a segment of time to focus our lives on the eternal God of the universe. We worship to draw on the strength and power of his presence to face the difficulties of life, as well as to express our thanksgiving. The word "sabbath" comes from an old Babylonian word which means "stop doing what you normally do." Every one of us needs to stop doing what he or she normally does in one's work and play and focus upon God so that each of us can draw the power of God's presence into our lives. We are a holy temple, the people of God gathered to worship. We need worship as surely as our eyes need light to see, our ears need sound to hear, our lungs need air to breathe, and the body needs food to sustain it.

The Foundation of Community

The Church is also a **community. It is a fellowship**. It is a group of people who reach out to one another to draw strength from each other. As Paul reminds us, "We are bonded and knit together, no longer aliens, strangers, but we are fellow citizens." We belong now to the community. We are not strangers; we are a part of the family. That is what the Church is — family.

I recall seeing a movie several years ago in which two prisoners, a black man, and a white man, were chained together in a prison camp. Anything they tried to do could not be done if they worked in discord. They had to learn to work in harmony. One day they escaped from the prison camp and, they learned quickly that if they were going to run, they had to do it together or else they would continuously fall. They were bonded together. Since we are bonded to the life of our neighbor, whether they are sister or brother, here in the fellowship of the Christian faith, we are involved in the lives of others. Our faith is always very personal, but it is never private. As a part of the Church, we live in relationship to others and never exist just in isolation. We reach out to others in their particular needs to show them that we care for them.

The Rebirth of the Church

I know something of the concern and community of this congregation which has reached out to touch the lives of many in this community and I hope it will spread even more. Some of you are not really a part of that kind of community yet. In the Sunday School classes, W.M.U. circles, youth groups, and sometimes in other kinds of organizations within this church, you find persons who have bonded together into a strong fellowship in the church. It is amazing to see what community has meant to the Church as individuals were knit together one to the other down through the centuries. It was the early Church community which nurtured Paul and commissioned him to found other communities. It was the Christian community which sustained him and to whom he later wrote his epistles. The Church never exists merely for individuals, but individuals bonded together in fellowship in the body of Christ.

In one of Charles Schulz's cartoons, Charlie Brown is sitting down watching television when Lucy enters the room and changes stations. He turns around and asks: "What gives you the right to change the station? I was watching that program!" She holds up her hand and says, "See these fingers. Individually they are not much, but when brought together like this, they become a force that's mighty to behold." Charlie Brown says, "That's reason enough."

When problems, difficulties, pains, aches, turmoil, demands, and hardships come upon us, they may be too much for us individually to withstand. The power of community helps us withstand these forces. When there is an awareness of each undergirding the other as a part of the fellowship of Christ, we sense the bond of togetherness which has knitted us together as a part of the Body of Christ. As "a building together," we can withstand the strain or difficulty because we do not attempt to stand there isolated or alone. We share them with a brother or sister, and we find the strength of the community of faith.

The Foundation of Concern

If we are *to* build the Church, there is also **the stone of concern and caring in its foundation.** If we are a Christian community, it means that we really care for one another. We cannot be concerned for one's own selfish ends, but we must learn to reach out and see the needs and demands of others. I am convinced that life teaches us early that caring is a very powerful emotion. We have signs all around us which remind us about the importance of caring. We see the sign when we pass on a two-lane road, "Pass with care." We used to send "care packages" during the Second World War. We talk sometimes about getting tender loving care and a lotion with that same name. We have, stamped on some of our packages, "Handle with care." I suppose one of the worst phrases that anybody can ever say to us is, "Well. I couldn't care less." But the Church is supposed to be a community that could not care more for one another. The Church is the place where we reach out to touch one another with our concerns and our needs.

As the body of Christ, the Church is like a web. When any one part is touched, the whole feels the vibration. When there is an ache which hurts over in this corner of the Church, another part senses it as well. We are attuned and knit together as a part of the body of Christ, and experience each other's needs and, then, seek to reach out with arms of love, support, and concern for one another. The authentic Church, then, is a community of caring people. The Church is concerned about the educated and the uneducated, the wealthy and the poor, the young and the old, the singles and the married. The Church addresses all kinds of needs. It reaches out to the sick and to the well, to those whose marriages are sound and to those whose marriages are trembling with discord. The Church reaches out to the ill and well, the lonely and happy, the grieving and the rejoicing, and the strong and weak. It says to all people we care for you. In this community the Church reaches out to express God's love and grace.

"We are a holy temple," the Scriptures declare. The word "holy" means to be set apart. We are set apart not for our own glory. We cannot go over into some private corner and say: "Oh, aren't we wonderful boys and girls and men and women." We are set apart to serve. To be Christ's people in the world means that we will be involved in the life of our own community where we care for one another. Where there is lack of caring and concern, we have to question whether that structure is really the Church.

The Foundation of Compulsion

Another foundation stone in the building of the Church is **a great sense of compulsion.** You and I cannot keep the gospel to ourselves, but we are commissioned to share it with other people. Emil Brunner says that "the Church exists by mission just as fire exists by burning." When a fire ceases to burn, it is not fire. When a church ceases to be concerned about other people, and stops sharing the good news of the gospel, it has become only a social club. Without a sense of compulsion to share the good news, the Church is not a part of the body of Christ. In Christ's name we are willing to go, to be, and to serve. In the Great Commission of Jesus, the statement is expressed in the Greek not as imperatives but as participles. It reads more exactly, "As you are going..." Jesus is assuming that those who have felt and experienced his redeeming grace will be sharing the good news with other people. Not to share the gospel is to leave the blind man in his darkness, the deaf person in her silence, the beggar at the gate, to pass by on the other side of the man hurt on the Samaritan Road, and to leave those who hurt in their pain.

We cannot be content to receive the good news, but we must also be willing to share it. We must not be content to receive salvation but to become agents of reconciliation. We must not be content to receive love but to become lovers in the world so that other people can see the power and grace of Christ through our lives. We must not be satisfied to accept the labor and sacrifices of our ancestors and be unwilling to labor in Christ's Church ourselves. In 2 Samuel 24: 19-25, we have the story where David approached a stranger, who was not a Hebrew, and asked him if he could buy a certain field and build an altar to God. The man offered to give the field to David, but David declined his offer, and said: "No. I will not offer to the Lord my God that which costs me nothing." We have to remember that it often can be costly to be a part of the community that worships God, and we do not want to offer God "that which costs us nothing." It is not "cheap grace," as Dietrich Bonhoeffer reminds us.

It will cost you and me time, energy, and possessions as we commit them in Christ's service. In the Church of Christ there is a sense of compulsion to go and share the good news of Christ with others. We are commissioned to build the Church of Christ. We are knitted together and bonded together as his people. The Church as "living stones" is a living, growing organism. The Church is always a living body because it is a living God who directs its mission.

A painting depicted Satan and Faust engaged in a chess match. Underneath the painting were written these words, "Checkmate." If you know anything about chess, you know that the word "checkmate" means the game is over. The king can make only limited moves, while the queen is the most versatile player on the board. Other pieces on the board have limited moves. One day a world champion chess player came into the art gallery and studied the painting for a long time, and, then, he exclaimed so that everybody in the gallery could hear him: "It's a lie. Both the king and the knight can move!"

There are a lot of people who are trying to tell us that the Church is dead; it is checkmated. That is a lie. The Church of Jesus Christ is alive and at work in the world. We are a part of his Church. We are the people of God. Let Christ build us, mold us, and make us into the kind of people that we should be. May God grant that we shall be his living Church in the world.

3
The Challenge of Change

Several years ago, a nine-year-old boy died of old age. He was suffering from *Progeria*, a disease described as rapidly advancing age. At nine years old he had all the symptoms of a person ninety years old. He was bald. His skin was very wrinkled. He suffered from hardening of the arteries and other difficulties of people in advanced age. You may have seen reports within the past few years on television or in the newspapers about several other young people who were suffering from this same illness.

I first read about this illness in Alvin Toffler's book, *Future Shock*. He used this boy as an example to describe the rapidity of change in its impact upon the world today. Just as a small nine-year-old boy seems to have lived ninety years within his short nine years, so many of us feel that time has been compressed by the changes which have taken place so quickly. It is difficult to adjust to the rapidity of the changes happening all around us in our world today. It is astounding what has happened so quickly. Look at the areas of medicine, science, and technology over the past few years. The changes that have occurred have been astronomical.

The Rapidity of Change

Two writers, Neil Postman and Charles Weingartner, have used the metaphor of a clock face to depict the changes which have happened within civilization. The sixty minutes on the clock represent the three thousand years since writing has been used. Each minute stands for fifty years. These two men then set some figures on that time clock, so we could see how close we are to many of the great events in world history. Only nine minutes ago on this kind of time clock, the Printing Press was invented. Three minutes ago, the locomotive, the telegraph, and the phonograph were invented. Two minutes ago, the radio, motion picture, rotary press, the telephone, the automobile, and the airplane were invented. The motion picture, which was invented just a few moments ago, added sound only a minute ago. Within the last ten seconds television and communication satellites were invented. Within the last five seconds computers came into existence; and within the last fraction of a second the laser, microchips, open-heart surgery, heart by-pass surgery, and transplants have been introduced. We are told that more has happened within the last split second scientifically, medically, technologically, and educationally than has taken place in all the rest of known history. And we wonder why we are shocked by the rapidity of the change all around us! Many simply do not know how to adjust to it at all.

I am old enough that I can remember the "B.T." days, "before television." There are days when we would all like to be free of television. Television, though, has rapidly changed our society. Our homes are often geared around it. Politicians now run their campaigns around television exposure. Many are elected because they are good at public relations and promotion and may be weak in political savvy or insight. It is the image that sells them. Television has changed sports, made it available for instant consumption, and holds an ideal of ability that will forever elude most of us. Television determines products we buy, where we go for vacations, clothes we wear, cars we ride in, and so many other things about our whole lifestyle. This is true even to the point of what has happened in religious services on television. Entertainment is now the chief religious sales pitch and, if we are not entertained, many feel that they have not had a religious experience with God.

The automobile has also changed our society. Our landscapes have mountains of old cars piled high. Cities have been built around automobiles. Courting habits have been changed by automobiles.

Businesses and their job markets are determined often by the accessibility of automobiles. Computers, e-mail, fax machines, cell and smart phones and other forms of technology have forever changed our lifestyles. Yes, our society has undergone a great deal of rapid change, and some of us really do not know how to adjust to them.

Snoopy is seen lying on his doghouse in a peanuts cartoon. The night is black; the stars are shining brightly. As he is looking up into the heavens he says, "I am always impressed by the constancy of the stars. It gives me a feeling of security to look up and know that the star I see will always be there. And will ..." Suddenly he sees a shooting star fall across the sky. In the next frame, you see Snoopy lying across the top of his doghouse with his head down and with a droopy look of dismay. We are beginning to discover that even the stars fall and do not last forever.

Some have exclaimed: "Alas, alas the times now are not what the times used to be!" That inscription was written six thousand years ago in Babylonia. Even then times were changing. One of the popular songs of a few years back declared: "The times, they are a-changing." It is difficult for us to imagine what people tomorrow will think about the changes that will take place in the tomorrows ahead of us.

WE OFTEN PREFER THE FAMILIAR AND FEAR CHANGE

What can we you and I, as Christians, do in response to all the changes that are going on around us? How do we react to them? Well, a lot of us, if we are honest, really prefer permanency and fear change. We really do not like change. We want the old shoes and comfortable clothing. We slip into them quickly when we get home at the end of a busy day. Some of us prefer antiques because we know the quality of the merchandise and something about the era in which they existed. We like the security and the sense of permanency in those items. We know their style, history, and value and feel at home with them. We cling to that which is familiar and identifiable.

Halford Luccock said that he once took his six-year-old daughter for an afternoon ride on a merry-go-round in a nearby park. After five rides, she turned to him and said: "I'd like to live on a merry-go-round!" A lot of us prefer the merry-go-round type of life. We prefer to move around in those familiar circles in which we are secure. We want schedules and routineness. We reach out for some kind of security blankets of orthodoxy, customs, or traditions that make us feel comfortable. We desire those things that make us feel secure. We prefer the old paths and traditions that we understand. And we often cling tightly to them. We hug the shore of familiarity.

But…our world today is feeling an earthquake; a tremor that is tumbling the familiar structures all around us. Everything permanent is being shaken loose. The ground seems to be reeling beneath our feet and the important things are passing out of our life. As the walls begin to crack and fall, some of us do not know which way to turn. We look for a toe-hold. We look for something to cling to. We search for some secure, snug harbor where we can put our anchor down and remain secure. We are often terrified and frightened by the changes and do not know where to go or what to do. As the poet, W. B. Yeats, says "All changed, changed utterly."

"Hold the old way" is the watch-word of this perspective. Too many of us are like the old farmer who was interviewed as he approached his ninetieth birthday. "I suppose there have been a lot of changes in your lifetime," noted the reporter. "There shor have been," the farmer replied, "and I've been agin every blasted one of 'em!" A lot of us are that way. We simply cannot stand the changes that are going on around us. We scorn the new and sanctify the old; criticize the different and cling to the familiar; reject the changes and reclaim the customary; throw over the unfamiliar and hold on to the traditional.

CHANGE IS AT THE HEART OF THE UNIVERSE

Change is indeed all around us and we do not know where to turn or where to go. But we need to realize that change is at

The Rebirth of the Church

the very heart of the universe itself that was designed by God who created it. When God created man and woman and placed them within the world, God created them for growth. On examination, we discover that man/woman and the whole universe are still in process of changing, growing, and becoming. Nothing is finalized or complete. When God looked upon creation, God said "Behold it is good." Creation was not perfect, not finished, not over. God said, "It is good."

A church pulpit seems solid. The pews people sit on in church seem solid. But we are told by scientists that they are really particles in motion. If we could put them under the proper microscope, we could see that in actuality they are in motion. Our bodies are all still in process of growing. As one cell is dying, a new one is coming into existence. The atom itself is energy in motion. For awhile scientists thought the atom was a fixed unit, but when it was split, a world was discovered inside of it, also. Heat and light are waves or particles in motion. Matter does not perish but changes. Everything is in process and is constantly changing, sometimes rapidly and sometimes slowly. All creation is continuously growing. And where there is no change, there is no growth. Growth does not come if there is no change. But change, life will and must.

SOMETIMES CHANGE IS PAINFUL

If you don't think you have changed, look at a picture taken ten years ago. We all change. Exercise produces for us some sense of pain, if we have not done much for a while, or if we engage in an exercise that we are not used to. You and I know that when we flex muscles that have not been used to being exercised, we feel the strain upon our body. Our first steps were painful. We stumbled and fell several times before we could walk. Learning comes through the discipline of time, energy, and mental abilities. Growth itself is sometimes painful. Pain is a part of life. Ernest Campbell, the late minister of Riverside Church in New York City, asked a friend once "How do you know whether you should be for change or not?" He answered directly: "If it hurts, it's good." Real change always produces some pain in our lives because it indicates our need for growth. We always experience pain when the radically new comes into our lives. It is almost always painful when something that is different from the routine crosses our path.

Many people have stood in the way of progress and have simply marked time and watched it march past them, because they have spent too much of their time clinging to the shore of the past and being unwilling to move toward the future. For some of us our motto is "Hang on to the old." Some ignore anything that is unfamiliar and hang on only to that which is certain and sure. Flexibility is a part of growth. Tall skyscrapers and high bridges are constructed to give a little in the wind. It is tragic indeed when life itself has built into it the whole process of change and growth and we choose instead the way of death-inflexibility.

When the great leader of Israel Moses died, God chose a new leader, Joshua. God confronted Joshua down by the River Jordan and said to him: "Moses, my servant is dead. Arise go over Jordan." Moses did a great work as a leader of Israel, but his time was now past. Joshua the new leader was challenged to arise and lead the nation even further. A pastor may serve faithfully a congregation for many years. His dedicated ministry can be affirmed, and the church will continue to build on his or her fine leadership. But, when that pastor leaves, the church will look to the coming of a new leader to guide them into the future.

CHANGE IS AT THE CENTER OF THE CHRISTIAN FAITH

The Christian insight is to see that we are committed not just to a dead past and what used to be but to the God who is marching on before us toward tomorrow. Let us seek to follow the God who is leading us into that which is yet to be. God's Spirit is guiding us forward to realize the potential as his people and his Church that God has for us to be. Change is the nature of the Christian faith.

Christianity has at its center an understanding of the newness of life. Repentance is at the very heart of our faith. We are challenged to turn from the old and turn to the Christ who gives us a new direction in life.

A NEW COVENANT

When we read the story from the book of Jeremiah (Jeremiah 31:31-34), the great prophet tells the people about the New Covenant that God is making with Israel. They had broken the old covenant, and they had rejected it because they had not remained faithful to God. God declared that He was giving them a new covenant which shall be written on their hearts. Jürgen Moltmann, a contemporary theologian, says that it might be better understood today to say that it was written on "our conscience." God writes upon our own conscience a sense of the newness that God has come to give us. As Christians we feel that it is in Jesus Christ that we find the new covenant fulfilled. It is a covenant placed in your heart and my heart by a vital relationship to the Lord Jesus Christ.

THE NEW CREATION

The change is radical. As Paul writes to the Corinthians, "The old has passed away, the new has come" (2 Corinthians 5:17-19). There is a new creation. Old things are passed away, behold they are becoming new." In divine newness, God brings transformation not destruction, renewal not obliteration. God's spirit transforms us into a higher form. This is seen most vividly in Paul's metaphor of planting of grain as a picture of the change of the Christian at the time of death from a material body to a spiritual body. "Behold I show you a mystery." (I Corinthians 15:35-50) Here is the ultimate transformation. We pass from the earthly to the heavenly, from the material to the spiritual.

Change Within and Without

The Christian faith has 'new' as a key word in its religion. We speak about a "new birth," a "new song," a "new commandment," a "new creation," and "renewal of spirit". Our faith is founded on newness and change within and without. When we seek the traditional way, we may be far from the spirit of the Christ who came to usher in the new covenant. To desire absolute security is not to understand the God who is constantly seeking to move us forward to be like the divine Creator. The world cannot be saved without being changed, and neither can we. Change begins with us as individuals.

You can't contain the new wine that Jesus Christ is seeking to give us in old wineskins. He says his presence will burst them. Jesus Christ is constantly disrupting old customs, constantly setting aside old traditions, deposing ancient creeds and beliefs, that we might see the newness, freshness, and vitality of His spirit and power in our world today.

God, the Agent of Change

I guess it was over fifty years ago that Harry Emerson Fosdick wrote that the commonest sin of Christians is respectability. Stagnation has no place in the Christian life. We think that the gospel has always got to be so orthodox or that it must be so traditional. We forget that God is continuously revising our traditions, and bringing new insights, new directions, and new ways of understanding who and what God is as the God of the universe. God is the agent of change. The "new creation" parallels the original creation in its radical change in our lives. God transforms our outlook, values, philosophies, theologies, systems, and nature.

In the Highgate Cemetery in London, England, there is a grave with the bust of Karl Marx on it with this inscription: "The philosophers have interpreted the world in various ways; the point however is to change it." We cannot leave all changing to communism. Jesus Christ came into the world not simply to interpret an old law, not simply to tell us about an ancient tradition, not simply to please everybody's orthodoxies, or so religious people could be satisfied or made happy. He came to bring something radically new in the world. He came to transform life and to bring us into communion and fellowship with the God whose love is radical in its demand upon us and in the kind of change it seeks to make in your heart and in mine. He didn't come to annihilate the old but to infuse it with a newness of life that no one had really experienced before. Change is always dangerous, but not to change leads to stagnation of spirit and perspective.

THE CHURCH IS FACING MANY CHANGES

The institutional church is facing many changes today. Some people will not like the changes that will occur. The church must project its ministry for the future. The church of tomorrow may not be the same church it is today. Some want the church to be a small community church that it once was years ago. Some want the church to go back and be like the church was in the fifties. But the church will never be like it was in the fifties again, or the sixties, seventies, eighties or nineties. The church must have a vision that will enable it to reach out into the cities, across the countryside, and across the land, to draw people into fellowship, service, and ministry for Christ.

We can't talk about clinging to the old ways of what we used to be like. Instead we need to open ourselves to the freshness and the vitality of what God is seeking to call us to be as God's people today. Our responsibility is to be God's Church today, not last week, not last month, not two years ago and not thirty years ago, but what we can be as God's people today is God's challenge to us. We have to open our spirits to God's spirit to experience the warmth and guidance of the divine presence as God goes before us. We can't go back, only forward. God doesn't always come into our lives to make us comfortable or secure. Sometimes God comes into our lives to make us very uncomfortable. God may challenge our security to motivate us to be pioneering, courageous, and adventuresome in service and ministry.

We have to be careful that we do not fall into the sin of thinking that we can confine God to our buildings. Ancient Israel knew that God could not be contained within their tents made of skins, and neither shall we contain God within our buildings. Our church buildings should be the place where we gather to worship God and seek to find ways to minister effectively for God in the city and community. But I believe that God is always calling us to be a pilgrim people. God calls us to go out into the world as agents of reconciliation. Having been reconciled by God, we now go into the world to touch others with the sense of the power, presence and love that has touched your life and my life. And go ... we must. We shall be God's pilgrim people who are seeking to go into the world with God's love. We lift our anchor and hoist our sails to follow God into the seas of life.

God Is Constant

Amid a world that is constantly changing, you and I rest our sense of assurance on the God who goes before us and who is the God who is constant. We sometimes sing: "0, Thou who changest not, abide with me!" We rest our assurance in a changing world on the one who abides forever. God is the perfect being. God is perfection. Our challenge is to be more like God. God calls us to reach beyond where we already are in our moral and spiritual growth. Jesus challenges us to be perfect as our Heavenly Father is. Although it is a goal that is always evasive and beyond our grasp, it is a goal that pulls us beyond who and what we have already realized to what we can become through the presence and power of Christ in our life.

Christ is the One who is from everlasting to everlasting. He is the One who is the same yesterday, today and forever. You and I can probably never adjust very well to change unless we are vitally related to the One who is unchanging --the eternal God of the universe. You and I cling to the assurance that we can depend upon God. Though we may not always understand God's spirit, and though we may not understand totally God's way of working in the world, we have a strong sense of assurance and competence in the unchanging One. We put our trust in God and know that God's peace strengthens us, that God's comfort comforts us, and that sometimes God's challenging spirit challenges us to live differently in the world.

Lloyd Douglas, author of *The Robe*, said once he went to visit a friend of his who was an old violin teacher. He said he enjoyed talking with this friend because he had a kind of homely wisdom which refreshed him. One morning Douglas entered his studio and asked: "What's the good news today?" His old friend reached over and picked up a padded mallet and hit his tuning fork which was suspended from a silken cord and said: "There's the good news for today. That, my friend, is the note 'A'. It was 'A' all day yesterday. It will be 'A' all day tomorrow and next week and for a thousand years. The soprano upstairs may warble off-key, the tenor next door may flat his high ones, and the piano across the hall may get out of tune. And there may be noise all around us. But that, my friend, is an 'A'. That is the good news."

The good news for you and me is that there is constancy in the presence and power of the God of our universe. We can have confidence because we have this presence and power in our lives. Although we know that we do not have the total knowledge of who God is and what God's will and purpose is, we have sufficient knowledge to enable us to live with assurance that our faith will sustain us. To be related to the One who is constant is good news for us.

A woman called her pastor and asked him to come see her father who was dying. He indicated he would come by as soon as possible. The daughter indicated to him that sometimes she would have to run to the store and she said, "I'll leave the door open. If there is no answer to your knock, just go on in. You'll find my dad's room is in the back." Later the pastor stopped by to visit the man.

He knocked on the door but there was no answer, so he went on through the house to the father's room. When he got to the room, he found a chair was pulled up close beside the bed. "Ah, you must have been expecting me," the minister said. "No," said the man, "the chair hasn't been put there for you. I've been having trouble praying, but a friend said if I would put a chair there for the Lord and pretend he was sitting there, I could talk to him more naturally. So, I placed a chair there and tried it, and it really works." "That's fine," said the minister. "Anything that is helpful is good."

A few days later, the woman let the pastor know that her father had died. He expressed his sympathy and asked if her father had died easily. "I think so," she said. "He had called me in to show me something in the funny papers and we both had a good laugh. Then, I went out to the store to get some milk and when I came back I found him dead."

"I'm glad your father's death was easy," said the minister. "There was just one strange thing," said the woman. "Oh?" said the minister. "Yes," she said, "apparently he had pulled a chair over to the bed and was struggling to get into it or to use it to stand up, because when I found him, he had put his head and shoulders over the chair and died with his head in it."

We can step into today, tomorrow, this century or the life that stretches beyond death with the assurance that God is there. We know we can trust God to be with us in the quest for meaning. We can place our life in the hands of Christ with the assurance that nothing separates us from the love of God. We know that Christ will be present to sustain us and guide us. This is the bedrock of our faith and even if change is all around us we have that assurance.

So, go forth as God's people in the world, unafraid of change, because we have within our lives the One who changes not. We need not fear the changes that will come in our church, community, or in our own lives because we have the assurance that nothing separates us from God's presence when we are in Christ Jesus, our Lord. So, let change come, and let us be a part of the change agent in the world as God works through us to carry on the ministry of reconciliation. Live always with the assurance that God is present with you and will make each of us secure.

4

IN THE POWER OF THE SPIRIT

In what has become a classic comic act, a famous Munich clown comes on a stage which is covered completely in darkness, except for a small circle of light from a streetlight. He begins to look around in the circle of light, and, after a while, a police officer comes up to the clown and asks, "What are you looking for?" The clown replies, "I lost my house key and I am looking for it." So, the police officer begins to help him search for it and spends a considerable amount of time looking around in the light. Then the police officer asks, "Are you sure you lost it here?" "Oh no," the clown replies, "I lost it over there." He points to a dark corner. "Then why are you looking for it here?" asks the police officer. "There is no light over there," the clown responds.

How many times have we seen this scene? We search or look only where there is light for the moment. Most of us want to remain in the safe, secure light. But the urgent need and appeal today is that we carry light into the dark corners, wherever men and women are. We cannot remain in the security of the light when there are many crying from the darkness for help. Acts 1:6-8 indicates that Christ has given "power" to his church to carry light into the darkened world. Let's look at that challenge.

THE CHURCH: GOD'S INSTRUMENT TO COMMUNICATE SALVATION

First, Christ indicated that the church had been given power to be God's instruments to carry salvation to the world. We are to go into the dark corners wherever humanity is and tell them the Good News of Christ. However, instead of being the transforming element within the world, the church often seems to be merely a reflection of the rest of society. Many people can see no distinction, whatsoever, between those within the church and those outside of it. Some wonder what difference a church makes in many communities, except for the building itself. If we merely reflect the rest of society, what is there different about the church?

It seems to me, that as we look at the New Testament, the very purpose of the church was to be the living, vital organism, which extended God's redemption into the world. The church was to be the vehicle, the instrument, to carry the message of salvation, which has already come into the world. We are to proclaim that the miracle has already happened. We will not share that message if we merely reflect the rest of the world.

EVERYONE HAS RESPONSIBILITY TO SHARE THE GOOD NEWS

The church cannot be God's instrument if we take the approach, "Let somebody else do it." If we are constantly trying to pass responsibility to someone else, and not assume any for ourselves, the work of the church can never get done. How many times do we sit around and say, "Oh, if only someone would do something about the awful conditions in the world." But, we ourselves are unwilling to become involved. It is not enough for us simply to say, "Let Mr. Jones do it, or Mrs. Brown, or let the preacher do it, or someone else." We cannot throw the load to somebody else. We, too, have responsibility.

Many are often like one of Charles Dickens' characters, Mr. Skimpool. His philosophy was, "I am not going to accept any responsibility, not even for myself. I pass it on to somebody else." Unfortunately, this seems to be rather typical of so many today within the church. We shift the responsibility for carrying out ministry to someone else. But, each of us has his/her load to bear.

FINANCIAL SUPPORT IS ESSENTIAL

The church can't be God's mission instrument in the world if it does not have the financial support of the people. We wonder sometimes why a church makes no greater impact. It cannot make much of an impact on the world when we feel like we can simply drop a dollar in the offering plate this Sunday, or a few weeks from now, and think that the church is really going to make much of a difference in the world.

A woman said to me one time, "I am simply going to give a little of my money here, and some of it there, and a little someplace else." Unfortunately, too many give a little, especially, to the church. As I told this dear lady, "If all our members did like she did, we would soon close the doors of the church quickly." The church needs the faithful tithes and offerings of its people if it is going to be about God's work. If the church is going to make an impact on the world, it must have the strong financial support of its people. Some people say, "If I don't like a certain little thing that is going on down there at the church, then I will not support it." Then why aren't you down there seeking to make something different? It is *your* church, not their church. Every single one of us needs to be a vital, dynamic, faithful supporter of the church.

THE CHURCH CANNOT BE FOCUSED PRIMARILY UPON ITSELF

The church can't be God's instrument if it is only introspective and spends its time looking at its "churchliness." When the church is only concerned about itself, with its building, pews, and furniture, it is not going to have much of an impact in the world. This is not to say that these things are not important. Of course, they are. However, the church needs to recapture its vision of what the church is. The building merely houses the Church. The Church has to go into the world as God's redemptive messengers. Our basic concern with ourselves is probably one of our greatest sins as a church.

Suppose, for example, that the local fire station decided that it would no longer answer fire alarms. Instead of fighting fires, the fire station was going to spend all of its time making the fire station look beautiful. They air-conditioned it, put in comfortable seats, painted their fire trucks to be the prettiest in town, and then spent their time polishing the trucks, and then they purchased the finest uniforms that they could have so they would look beautiful. When a fire alarm alerted them that a house was burning down, suppose they simply sat around and polished the fire truck instead of answering the call. Would we think that they were doing their job? They certainly would have missed their basic purpose for existing.

The church, unfortunately, could be like a fire station. We gather every week to prepare ourselves to go into the world to do God's mission. The church is the arm of redemption to bring transformation within the world. We are charged not merely to take care of ourselves, but to utilize our buildings and everything we have to do God's work in the world. We do our job, only as we go into the world.

THE CHURCH ADVANCES WHEN IT IS MISSION MINDED

Second, as we examine the history of the church, the periods of its greatest growth, and the time that the church seemed to have made the most impact through the centuries, has been during the time when it was a missionary church. It seemed to grow when it was concerned for others. Jesus told his disciples to go into the world. They began right in Jerusalem, and then moved to Judea, to Samaria, and then to the outermost parts of the world. As they carried this message forward, the church came into being and others were attracted to it. While Judson, Livingston, Cary, Schweitzer, Lottie Moon, Bill Wallace, and other great missionaries were involved in their work, the church made a great impact on the world. To be unconcerned about the rest of the world, and only concerned with itself, will bring about the demise of the church.

I saw a painting, not long ago, about a dead church. It wasn't some little country church, which had fallen down and had been deserted by its members. Do you know what the artist painted? He painted a huge building, a giant cathedral, filled with people. These people were singing with gusto, the pews were packed. But, the mission box in the back of the church was covered with dust and cobwebs. The artist was trying to indicate that the church was only concerned with itself, and not with sharing the Good News with others. That church is dead!

MOTIVES FOR MISSIONS

Third, the contemporary church will have power when it has the proper motives for missions. Let me suggest a few.

THE LOVE OF CHRIST

I think our first motive is the one that comes to us from the love of Christ. We love because He first loved us. We are able to love other people when we have been properly loved. We are told that children, who have never been loved by their parents, can never really love somebody else. You and I should be able to be the extension of God's love into the community, because we have sensed God's love through Jesus Christ, and God's great sacrifice for us.

THE COMMISSION OF CHRIST

A second motive is the commission we have from Christ. I believe that the best translation of the Great Commission from Jesus is "as you are going, you will be teaching; you will be preaching, you will be baptizing ... "(Matthew 28:19). Jesus assumed his disciples would be going. We have a commission from Christ to share the Good News with other persons, no matter where we see them.

A young secretary was startled one day as her boss said to her, "Oh yes, I know, you belong to that funny little church." At first his comment made her rather mad, but, then, as she thought about it awhile, she responded to him by saying, "Well, I am glad that my 'funny little' church shows."

I wonder, now in all seriousness, if anybody has the foggiest notion that you and I belong to any church, especially our personal local church. Do they see a distinction in your life, and mine, and what this church means? We are to be the redemptive element in society — to share the Good News of Jesus Christ with others. Have they seen that in your life, and in mine?

HUMAN NEED

A third motive comes from our awareness of human need. Wherever we see men and women in need, that is where we want to share the Good News of Jesus Christ. One of my former churches engaged in a local mission project called "Inasmuch". This mission emphasis was based on Jesus' statement "Inasmuch as you have done it to the least of these, you have done it unto me" (Matthew 25:40). On a selected Saturday, children, young people, adults, and senior adults met to carry meals to needy families, do repairs in the homes of elderly members who were unable to do them, paint the Boys' and Girls' Club, deliver firewood to furnish fuel for a family, visit some persons in the local nursing homes, help stock the pantry of a local food shelter, do repairs in a local Girl's Home, and many other hands-on projects. These persons touched the lives of many others that day. We saw some needs in our community and attempted to meet these needs in some small way. Wherever the needs are, we were seeking to bring about a response. Whenever we as Christians meet human needs, we enable these persons to sense Jesus' concern for them and open them to the power of Christ's redemption. As Emil Brunner, the great German theologian, once said, "Just as fire exists by burning, so the church exists by mission." When the church loses its sense of mission, it loses its reason for being.

The Rebirth of the Church

CALLED TO SERVE

A fourth motive is to be of service, like our Lord. Jesus said, "The greatest of all is the servant of all." We seek to serve wherever we are. All our "Inasmuch" ministries were a means of taking a cup of cold water, visiting the sick, and showing concern to others. Our goal is not to lift up ourselves, but to find ways to glorify and serve our Lord. This means that, sometimes, we have to get our hands dirty. The Christian faith is a cross-like way of living. The real Christian faith is concerned with getting our hands dirty as we reach down where there is human need. We are not merely called to look, but to do, and to be.

One of the groups that worked with our church members in the "Inasmuch" emphasis was from the Odum Home in Pembroke, North Carolina. This group of young men helped us in the loading and distribution of firewood. One of the workers from the Odum Home told me that he hoped, one day, that he would be able to go to medical school. He wanted to be a pediatrician. He said he wasn't sure if he wanted to be a medical missionary, or to find a place here in our own country to serve. He asked me which I thought he should do. My only reply to him was that he needed to understand his own sense of calling. He could serve God as a medical missionary, but he could also serve God effectively, and maybe even more effectively, as a physician who gives his life in dedicated service wherever he is. We don't have to be professional holy persons to serve God. We can serve God through whatever vocation we have in life if we are willing to put first God's kingdom. We can serve and witness for Christ at work, at home, in our leisure and wherever we are.

I know you have all seen copies of the beautiful painting of Christ standing before a door knocking with a lantern in his hand. This painting is based on the famous one by Holman Hunt. Two men were standing before the original painting by Holman Hunt one day. One of the men, as he looked at the lantern in the hand of Jesus said, "I can't understand why Jesus has that lantern in his hand. There is plenty of light there. He doesn't need that lantern at all." A man standing behind him responded, "I couldn't help but overhear your comment. Notice that on one side of the painting, Mr. Hunt has painted a wilderness, which is dark. I think the idea in the painting is that when Jesus Christ comes into the house of people with the lantern, the people are then to take that light into the dark wilderness, and tell others about Jesus Christ, who is the light of the world."

The church, indeed, exists by mission. Whenever we lose our sense of mission, we have lost our reason for being. God will empower us to take the light into the dark world when we commit our lives more fully to doing what God would have us do in the world.

5
THE TASK OF THE CHURCH TODAY

Several years ago, the archbishop of Canterbury wrote a circular letter to his priests and asked if they would meet him in London for a "quiet day." One of his priests wrote back, "What my church needs is not a quiet day but an earthquake!" There are a lot of churches that need an earthquake in them. The words of the "Great Commission" from Matthew's Gospel (28:16-20) have shaken the church like an earthquake down through the centuries. These words have continuously reminded the church of its task, its missionary purpose, and its call to evangelism.

Let us begin by looking at the setting of the passage in Matthew 28:16-20. Our story takes place after Jesus had been raised from the dead. The disciples went to a mountain to meet Jesus. We know that the eleven disciples were there. But Paul tells us in one of his epistles (I Corinthians 15:6) that over five hundred persons were gathered there. Suddenly Jesus appeared to the disciples and they worshipped him. He came among them as a conquering Lord--a victorious king. Jesus appeared to the disciples and five hundred others on a mountain in Galilee. He told them their responsibility and their missionary task. This charge has echoed through the chambers and heart of the church through the centuries. Note its message for us today.

A TREMENDOUS CLAIM

Jesus begins with *a tremendous claim*. Jesus said, "'All authority on heaven and on earth has been given to me'" (Matthew

28:18). Who is this that makes such a stupendous claim? Isn't this the one who was a Galilean peasant, the man who worked until he was thirty as a carpenter in Nazareth? Isn't he the one who said that he didn't even have a place to put his head down at night? Wasn't he just a penniless, itinerant preacher? Where are his armies? Where is his political power? Where is his wealth?

Yet Jesus claimed, "All authority has been given to me." What authority? All authority in heaven and on earth. It is the same kind of authority that he taught us to pray for in the Lord's Prayer that God's will "be done on earth as it is in heaven."

Jesus claimed that this authority had been placed in his hands by his Father. How did he get it? "All authority has been given to me," Jesus declared. Matthew began his gospel by introducing Jesus as the Son of David and the Son of Abraham. This same Jesus was listed in a Jewish genealogy and was crucified with an inscription over his cross, "The King of the Jews." This Jesus, after the resurrection, is declared sovereign Lord of all the universe.

This claim echoes through the New Testament. Paul writes that the glorified Christ when raised from the dead was seated at the right hand of the Father in heavenly places and "is far above all rule and authority and power and dominion, and above every name that is named, not only in this age but also in that which is to come; and he has put all things under his feet" (Ephesians 1:20-21). Again, in another place he wrote that Jesus was "designated Son of God in power according to the Spirit of holiness by his resurrection from the dead" (Romans 1: 4). When Jesus was raised from the dead, his disciples sensed something about his power which they had not realized before the crucifixion. Listen to Paul again: "Christ emptied himself, taking the form of a servant he humbled himself and became obedient unto death on a cross. Therefore, God has highly exalted him and bestowed on him the name which is above every name, that at the name of Jesus every knee should bow, in heaven and on earth and under the earth, and every tongue confess that Jesus Christ is Lord, to the glory of God the Father" (Philippians

The Rebirth of the Church   51

2:7-11). "He is above all things, and in him all things hold together" (Colossians 1:1 7).

Peter wrote in his epistle, "Through him you have confidence in God who raised him up and gave him glory" (1 Peter 1:21). The writer of the Epistle of Hebrews declares, "We see Jesus, who for a little while was made lower than the angels, crowned with glory and honor because of the suffering of death" (Hebrews 2:9). The writer of the Book of Revelation asserts that "Worthy is the Lamb who was slain, to receive power and wisdom and might and honor and glory and blessing!" (Revelation 5:12). The Scriptures affirm that this Jesus Christ is One unto whom all authority has been given. His resurrection was the sign and mark of the· approval of God on his ministry.

What territorial rights does Jesus have? Lord of what? Jesus claims all. When he stands before the door of a person's heart and knocks, he expects that individual to give him all of his or her life. This Lord, having been obedient unto death and having been raised from the grave by God, reigns triumphantly and now comes to us and challenges us to follow him and his way. He demands control of the material, mental and moral areas of our life.

The amazing thing is that persons down through the ages have given him authority and power in their lives. Kings have knelt and taken their oath in his name. Presidents in our country lay their hands on a Bible and pledge their oath in his name. Rulers have gone forth under the banner of his cross to claim new territories. Others have given their lives in sacrifice to spread his good news around the world. Hospitals, universities, homes for children and the elderly have been established under his authority. Artists, writers, poets, musicians — every realm of life — has been touched by his authority. No area is free from his influence.

Christ comes into the life of a person and touches their life and demands obedience. He knocks at the door of a person's life. Unfortunately, many are like the poor woman who could not pay her rent. One day she heard a knock at her door. The knock continued. It grew louder, but she continued to ignore it. Later when her pastor, who had come with money to pay her rent, asked why she did not respond, she said she thought it was the landlord who had come to collect the rent money. She did not realize that the one who was knocking had come to pay her rent.

Jesus Christ continues to come knocking at the door of every person's heart. Some of us draw back fearing that this summons is a call to "pay the rent." However, Jesus has come to give us a gift--redemption. We are afraid to respond because we think we may be demanded to pay something. Jesus approaches us not demanding a payment but with the good news that he has already paid for us through his sacrificial death. His sacrifice draws us to himself and he summons us to respond to his call to discipleship.

Two thousand years ago there was a man who was seen leaning over his tax ledger. He was restless and depressed. He knew that he had been rejected by his friends. He was a Jew who was collecting taxes from his Jewish friends and neighbors for the Roman government. But one day a shadow fell across his table. He looked up and recognized that Jesus of Nazareth cast the shadow. He had heard this preacher before. He had been moved deeply by him. But ... But could he, a person who was despised and rejected by his own Jewish people, find a new beginning? Then Jesus said to Matthew, "Come, follow me." The man who was later the author of one of the gospels laid down his tax ledger, got up, and followed Jesus Christ. His life was forever changed.

Jesus Christ made an audacious claim. "All authority in heaven and on earth has been given to me." He approaches your heart and mine and knocks at that door, and you and I are summoned to respond. We cannot always explain our surrender to this claim. We are grasped by it and only those who participate in it really understand this claim.

A Great Commission

Go a step further with me as we look at Matthew 29:16-20 and you will see that there is not only a tremendous claim, but

The Rebirth of the Church

Jesus also gives the church a ***great commission.*** Here he presents to us our task, our responsibility as his church. Jesus begins in verse nineteen by saying, "Go therefore and make disciples of all nations, baptizing them in the name of the Father, Son and Holy Spirit and teaching them to observe all that I have commanded you." It is a shame that we do not have a verb "disciple" in English. The principle verb is disciple--make disciples. The going, baptizing, and teaching are subordinate to make disciples. Disciple is a verb, an imperative. Everything that precedes and follows "make disciples" is subordinate to it. Literally it reads, "As you are going, as you are baptizing, as you are teaching, you will make disciples." You will be discipling persons who will commit their lives to the authority of Jesus and learn and grow under his teachings.

Several summers ago, my family rented a place at the beach. One of the problems that you can have at a beach cottage is ants. Something sweet was accidentally dropped on the floor in the kitchen. A message went forth. Soon a whole host of ants had gathered around that sweet savory item. When I saw the ants gathered there with their long line extended from their home base, I thought about the church. Why can't we, with such a marvelous message, go forth and share that great news with others. Shouldn't there be a signal going out to those around the church to come and savor the good news of the gospel? Let us be about that business.

I recently read that if someone shared gossip with two other persons and they in turn with two others and those two with two more and on and on, it would theoretically take less than eight hours for every person in the world to hear that bit of gossip. If every Christian shared the Good News with two others and those with two each and on and on, soon the whole world would hear about Jesus Christ. We have to share the message with others.

Jesus Christ left ***an unmistakable imperative*** for his followers. "Go therefore and make disciples of all nations. (Matthew 28:19). Jesus told his first disciples: "Follow me and I will make you fishers of men" (Mark 1:17). Our Lord acknowledged that the need was great, and more evangelists were essential to accomplish his mission. "The harvest is plentiful, but the laborers are few; pray therefore the Lord of the harvest to send out laborers into his harvest" (Luke 10:2). "You shall be my witnesses" (Acts 1: 8). This was the charge our risen Lord gave to his disciples. The mandate of our Lord is clear-- his disciples have been commissioned to be evangelists.

But even when we affirm that mandate from our Lord, many of us are not clear how to do the work of an evangelist or we are turned off by the fanatical or arrogant personalities of a few professional or lay evangelists. It is unfortunate that many have let distorted or objectionable persons or methods keep them from doing what our Lord has challenged his disciples to do.

Evangelism is a beautiful New Testament word. The English noun evangelism contains the word "angel." An angel is a messenger who brings good news about God. That's what an evangelist is. It is a person bringing to another the good news about God's revelation and redemption through Jesus Christ. Let us not let the distorted images keep us from doing what our Lord has charged us to do.

Jesus said, "Disciple all nations." The *"all"* indicates the wide horizon of the evangelistic message of Christ. Christ was concerned and is concerned with all persons, classes, ages, races, and sexes. Paul writes in his Ephesians letter about the dividing wall that separated Jews and Gentiles in the temple. The Jewish temple was composed of an exterior Court of the Gentiles; next the Court of the Women, then the Court of the Israelites for the men, next the Court of the Priests, and finally the Holy of Holies. Paul declared that the death of Jesus had broken down all these dividing walls. Christ brought an end to barriers. Persons could come directly to God.

Unfortunately, too many walls still exist today. Thankfully, the Berlin Wall and the Iron Curtain which separate nations have fallen. But barriers still exist. There are barriers-- walls-- between classes, nations, and colors. But Jesus has brought peace and unity. He broke down all these barriers. Rather than being exclusive, Jesus' message was one of inclusiveness. Jew or Greek, barbarian or intellectual, cultured or uncouth, male or female, rich or poor, young or old, conqueror or conquered, white or black, red or yellow, slave or free-- all persons are welcome in Christ's Kingdom. The commission to disciple all nations reminds us of the unlimited horizon of the Christian Church. Christ extends his love to all persons.

The first missionaries which the early church sent out were Paul and Barnabas. The trail of missionaries has continued for two thousand years. The 18th and 19th centuries have seen some of the greatest missionary pioneers. William Carey went to India in 1782; Robert Morrison to China in 1807; Adoniram Judson to Calcutta in 1812; Robert Moffat to Africa in 1818; David Livingstone to Africa in 1841; J. Hudson Taylor began the China Inland Mission in 1853; John G. Paton went to the New Hebrides in 1859; Lottie Moon to China in 1873; Bishop William Taylor to Africa in 1884; E. Stanley Jones to India in 1907; Albert Schweitzer to Lambarene, Africa in 1913; Mother Teresa began her work in 1946 and Dr. William Wallace was martyred in China in 1950.

The greatest challenges before us today come from the Muslim, Hindu, and Buddhist religions and the gods of materialism and sexism, our contemporary Baals. It is predicted that by the middle of the next century at the current rate of conversions there will be more Muslims than Christians in our country. That should challenge us to do our missionary task.

Several years ago, at the BWA Congress in Argentina, I heard one of our small sister European nation's note that it was now sending missionaries to the United States. We are seen as a needy mission field. How true that is when we note how many persons claim to believe in God but have never darkened the doors of church or bear witness in any way for their faith. At the feet of Christ, the redeemer, persons of all races can meet. The arms of Jesus Christ are extended to them in welcome, love, forgiveness, and acceptance.

Next Jesus said, "***Baptize*** them in the name of the Father, Son and Holy Spirit." Name stands for person. When you are baptized in someone's name that means that you now belong to them. You are bought with a price. You are now his property. You belong to Christ. You are his person.

Persons are to be baptized in the name of the Father, Son and Holy Spirit. This is one of the earliest references to the Trinity. To be baptized into "the name of the Father, Son and Holy Spirit" symbolized the surrounding--all-encompassing--nature of the triune God we worship. The baptized Christian is like a glass which is submerged in water. There is water inside of it and there is water surrounding it. We are both surrounded by God and filled with his presence. When we are baptized, our total being is surrounded by the reality of God's presence as we have known him as Creator, Redeemer, and Spirit. To recognize God as creator is to affirm God as the one who creates and sustains life. As the incarnate Son, he makes us whole and complete. As Spirit, he guides and directs our lives.

Then Jesus said his disciples were to go into the world *"teaching."* When you make disciples, the disciples must constantly be taught. Continuous education is essential to grow in grace. Jesus didn't say "to make disciples and let them stay where they entered the kingdom." Instead he commissioned us to "teach" them. The Church is charged to develop those whom they have evangelized into mature Christians. This requires instruction, pastoral nurture, worship, fellowship, and prayer.

But the primary emphasis on teaching is to teach obedience to Jesus' commandments. The emphasis is not to teach a creed but to teach conduct, not something to be believed but to be done. "Teaching them to observe all that I have commanded you." Having met Jesus Christ as Lord, what we learn from him is most important for us in how we live and not merely in what we believe. He has given to the church a great commission.

Several years ago, Emily and I spent the night at Shakertown at Pleasant Hill, Kentucky. Shakertown is the site where a small sect called Shakers settled when they migrated to America from England during the colonial period. Their name was given to them by observers who noted their religious practice of shaking vigorously

The Rebirth of the Church

during their worship to rid their body of sins. The Shakers practiced celibacy and, if a family converted to the Shakers, the family had to split up and the women and girls lived separated on one side of the "dorm" and men and boys on the other. Only minimal dialogue took place between the sexes.

The Shakers believed in hard work, stringent living, efficient methods of labor and, therefore, their farms prospered. Since they did not marry, and two thirds of the children left when they became adults and were given a choice, the number of the Shakers continued to grow small until the last surviving Shaker at Pleasant Hill died in 1903. Earlier when their numbers were larger, their only method of trying to reach others came when visitors sat in rows along the side of the wall in the "Meeting House" and watched the Shakers sing and "dance" or "shake" in worship. The minister observed them from a small window upstairs and came down after the service was over and talked with anyone who indicated interest in joining them.

The Shaker furniture, some of their buildings with their unique architecture and songs have survived. Their faith died, however, because they failed to pass it on. A cloistered faith, shut off from the outside world, cannot reach others. This danger is always with the church. We may have lovely buildings, furnishings, beautiful hymns, eloquent sermons, but if we do not share our faith with others outside our buildings, we may, like the Shakers, leave empty buildings and lovely furniture and songs with no one to pass on our faith. We have been given a great commission. We must not forget that.

For many Christians, the phone seems to be off the hook, disconnected, or not "buzzing" to their missionary task. We must not turn a deaf ear or pretend we cannot hear Christ's great commission to us. We are all charged to share the Gospel message with others.

A Continuous Presence

But go with me further into this text and note that Jesus has given us a ***continuous presence***. "Lo," Jesus said, "I am with you always to the close of the age." Here in this verse we find first a ***personal presence***." I **am** with you." "I am" echoes through the Gospel of John. Jesus said, "I am the Light of the world." "I am the Bread of life." "I am the true vine." "I am the way, the truth, and the life." "I am the resurrection and the life." "Before Abraham was I am." "I am the bright and morning star." "I am the good shepherd." "I am the door to the sheep." The "I AM" in this passage indicates the continuous presence of Jesus with us.

Marc Lovelace was a professor of archaeology, whom I studied under at Southeastern Baptist Theological Seminary, at Wake Forest, North Carolina. He gave an interesting interpretation about the passage in the third chapter of Exodus where God responded to Moses' question, "Whom should I say has sent me?" God's reply was: "Tell them that 'I AM THAT I AM' has sent you." Dr. Lovelace said that some ancient tablets which had recently been unearthed and deciphered by some archaeologist could translate the Hebrew words as "I SPEAK" as well as "I AM." "Tell them that I who speak sent you." This emphasis stresses that God not only is, but God Communicates with us. Jesus Christ is not only one who was, but he is here now. We can feel his power today and can communicate continuously with him.

An Abiding Presence

Jesus is not only a personal presence but is also an abiding presence. "Lo I am with you always." "All the days" is a literal translation of this word. Jesus is present with us not only on good days but bad days, when you are happy or sad, when you are sorrowful or filled with joy, on gray days or bright days when you are suffering or healthy. God is with you when you have a strong faith, or it is weak, when you feel religious or when you have all kinds of

The Rebirth of the Church

questions and doubts. No matter where you are in life's pilgrimage, God is present with you.

Let us remember that even on the darkest, foggiest day God is present. The fog may sometimes seem thick and heavy. We cannot always see the sun behind the clouds on a foggy day, but we know that it is still shining. Remember that even when you can't "feel" God's presence, God is still there. God is present whether we feel it or not. Christ continues to abide with his disciples and bears us up through all our difficulties, struggles, dreams, hopes, and longings. We do not face the world alone but are sustained by a presence that never forsakes us. God is always with us.

Imagine yourself sitting by a phone and seeing persons somewhere who are waiting to receive your call: a child away from home; a parent living alone; a friend isolated and alone; a father waiting to take his wife to the hospital for their first child; a person in pain or in need of a doctor. You can provide that responsive call. Imagine those persons across the seas who long to hear a response to the call for help in their loneliness, illness, lack of education and agricultural knowledge and search for meaning, and to know that God loves them and cares about them. They long to hear the Gospel. Let us make those calls through our love, words, deeds, and witness.

A Triumphant Presence

Finally, Jesus said, "Lo I am with you always to the close of the age." Jesus is also a ***triumphant presence***. Many peer into crystal balls, study the stars or cards, inquire of fortune tellers, or use other means to try to predict the future. We are not sure how history will end, but the Christian teaching is that God is in control of history. However, history ends, God is in charge of it. Christ will be triumphant. History will not end with a whimper or bang. God is the source and power behind our history. Jesus is depicted as a conquering Lord who will sit in final judgment on history. Christ will be present to the close of the age.

Sometimes we sing: "I Love to Tell the Story." We often sing this hymn with enthusiasm. I hope that you really do love to tell the story and that you will indeed tell the gospel story to others. Tell them about the beautiful story of God's love in Christ. All of us are needed in the missionary challenge. Some of us might go and serve as missionaries. All of us can pray and give our money to support others to go where we cannot go. Our financial support can aid missionary doctors and nurses, teachers, pastors, evangelists, agricultural workers, and many others.

There is an ancient legend about the time when Jesus returned to heaven and the angel Gabriel asked him about his plans on earth for continuing his work. Jesus said, "I have chosen twelve ordinary men to be my disciples." Then the archangel asks: "But what if they fail?" Jesus said, "I have no other plan."

We are his disciples — learners — but let us remember that we are also apostles-- those who have been sent to share the marvelous good news of Christ with all persons. We must not fail! The church proclaims boldly that Jesus Christ is Lord of lords and King of kings. Having made a tremendous claim of authority, Jesus has given his church a great commission. To share the good news of Christ is your task and mine as members of Christ's church. The continuous presence of Christ will inspire, strengthen, motivate, and guide our witness for him.

6

THE CHURCH NOBODY KNOWS

"The Church," a woman said to a friend, "Is no longer related to the first century and does not speak to our own." That is a rather tough indictment of the Church, because it says in effect that the Church is both unbiblical and irrelevant.

E. Stanley Jones, the famous missionary to India, told about a fort that he once saw which stood on a high hill in central India. That fort was once the center of power and authority for that federal state, but that power shifted to the secular city up the valley. Armed guards continued to walk around the fort with huge spears in their hands as though they were guarding a fort that still had some purpose. But it no longer had any authority. He never could figure out why they marched around it. They were guarding a fort that no longer had a purpose. It was totally irrelevant.

Some are saying that the Church is much like that today. It is both unbiblical and irrelevant. When it is unbiblical, it is cut off from its roots. When it is irrelevant, it has no fruits. The Church is going through a transition. I still have a great vision for what the Church can be and do. I have drawn this vision from the New Testament, especially from the teachings of Jesus and Paul's letter to the Ephesians. The Church which the New Testament describes is a Church that nobody knows. It may well be a church very unlike our churches today. It will demand of us a radical new understanding, new commitments, and new possibilities. If the church is to be both biblical and relevant, then "the church that nobody really knows" must become a reality. Let us examine some of these images from Paul's Letter to the Ephesians.

NOT AFRAID OF CHANGE

The Church that nobody knows will be a church that is unafraid of change. To be unafraid of change will be radically new for the church, because often the church has been the institution to instruct everybody "to toe the line." "This is where you must stand and how tall you may sit," it has often declared. The institutional church has forcefully stated: "This is what you have to believe." The Church built its theological fences with the Apostles Creed, the Nicene Creed, the Chalcedonian Creed, and other statements to declare what was the "true" faith. Some have traced our Baptists' theological roots back to The London Confession, The Philadelphia Confession, The New Hampshire Confession or The Baptist Faith and Message. "Here are our beliefs," we are told. This is how we must understand God. Toe the line.

Bertrand Russell, the famous agnostic once wrote: "I say deliberately that the Christian religion as organized in the churches has been and still is the principal enemy of moral progress in the world." That's a stinging indictment against the church. But remember it was the church that condemned Galileo as a heretic because he dared to give a new interpretation of science that differed with the teachings of the church of his day. It was the church that did, and still does in some quarters, condemn Darwin for his teaching about evolution. The church has often been the one institution that has stood in the way of new insight in many areas. There are some churches today that declare that man never landed on the moon. Their understanding of the Bible says that it couldn't be possible. Often the church has condemned, retreated from, or ignored the world.

The Church that nobody knows will be the church unafraid of change, because it will be like the church that Jesus established. When Jesus began his ministry, he was immediately confronted by the scribes and Pharisees who condemned anyone who violated their rigid traditions, laws, and customs. Their way was the only way men/women could worship God. But Jesus said, "It has been

The Rebirth of the Church

said unto you, but now I say unto you." Jesus came to bring a new birth, to give us a new covenant, a new song, and a new commandment. He cut through the religious rigidity of his day to bring new and fresh insight into God's love and way. The early church almost died in Jerusalem, because the disciples attempted at first to make the new converts Jews. If they had succeeded, Christianity would have been only a sect of Judaism. Their narrow, rigid, and authoritarian approach could have spelled the end of the new movement by Jesus. Fortunately, the Apostle Paul had deeper insight into the kind of Church Jesus had founded.

The Church that nobody knows will not be an unadaptable and rigid church but will seek to follow its Lord in whatever path he will lead them. As the Apostle Paul said, "If anyone is in Christ, he is a new creation; the old has passed away, behold, the new has come" (2 Corinthians 5:17). Any organism that is not growing dies. When growth ceases, the organism is dead. If the church does not seek to grow "to the measure of the stature of the fullness of Christ;" as Paul described in the fourth chapter of Ephesians, then it is in the process of dying.

I put some startling lines on our church bulletin cover several years ago: "The Seven Last Words of The Church: We Never Did It That Way Before." The seven last words reflect inflexibility, unwillingness to face the new, rigidity, heels dug in, unwillingness to let the Lord lead us into new forms of worship, new possibilities for ministry, new ways of being church. The Church nobody knows will not be a church like that but unafraid of change. Whenever the true church really follows Christ, it is willing to walk on the edge of heresy to follow the Lord into new truth. When God created us, God put our eyes in the front of our head and not in the back, so we could look ahead to new possibilities and not spend all our time looking back where we have been. The Church nobody knows will be a church unafraid of change.

Lay Leadership

The Church nobody knows will also be a church that will be predominately led by the ministry of the laity. In his Letter to the Ephesians Paul states this truth very clearly. "And these were his gifts: Some to be apostles, some prophets, some evangelists, some pastors and teachers, to equip God's people for work in his ministry" (Ephesians 4:11-16). Forget the comma that is placed after "to equip God's people" in the King James Version and in some other translations. The pastor and teacher are to equip all Christians for ministry. The ministry is not left into the hands of a few professionals. God has not left his ministry to a few holy professional persons. He has called the pastors and teachers to train and equip others for their service. There will always be a need for some people to go to seminary and be trained for leadership roles, but we have the emphasis in the wrong place when we seek to become so specialized and professional that we forget that the church was founded by and needs to be predominately led by lay persons. St. Matthews Baptist Church had a vision to erect a building that would be adequate until the year two thousand. If... if ...IF we really understood what the church of Jesus Christ were like and our ministry in that church, we could not contain the people that would be in that building in a few months after it was finished. In the Church of Christ, you ... you ... YOU and I are called to ministry — not to be spectators and sit. We are called to be witnesses in the world, to bring men and women to Christ. Everyone is a minister. The Church nobody knows is the church that will be predominately lay led. The church will rediscover that every single Christian is a minister. Everyone has his or her place of service. No one can be in the spectator stands. Everyone is involved in the game of life. The professional ministers are the trainers to equip, the playing coaches, the supervisor who works on the job. But the ministry in the world is to be done by everybody not just a few.

The church came into existence through laypeople. Jesus himself was a layperson — a carpenter. He was not a professionally trained rabbi. He went into the world preaching his message of God's love and drew around him other lay persons. Remember the twelve apostles were not professionally trained religious persons. They were all lay persons. The Apostle Paul was a rabbi, but he always earned his living by making tents. He was in effect a bi-vocational pastor. Barnabas, Stephen the first martyr, and all the rest of the Christians in the young Church went into the world as lay persons to share the new life they had experienced in Christ. Think of the challenge before them. When Jesus Christ ascended, there were only 120 known Christians in a country of four million persons. What word do you say to these people? The odds are too great! Forget it. It's hopeless. What can 120 persons possibly do to share the gospel of Christ in a country of four million? What did they do? They turned the country upside down. Christ had so changed their lives that they shared this good news with others.

Suppose the Apostle Paul had been a great believer in polls. Someone may have taken an ancient Gallup Poll in his day in the city of Ephesus and reported to him the following findings: "63% of the people worship Zeus; 12% worship Diana; 10% worship Mercury, and the other 10% don't worship at all." "They couldn't give a rip about religion," the pollster says. "Oh, by the way, there are two or three Christians here." Just think — two or three Christians among millions of people. But Paul didn't pay any attention to polls. He was overcome by the Gospel and felt such a sense of commission that he went into all the world to share the good news of Christ. This lay church will recognize the gifts of women as well as men in ministry. They will see that each person discovers his or her gift or calling and finds his or her place in service to utilize those gifts. It will recognize persons of all races and sexes and help them develop their gifts to serve Christ.

A Whole Ministry

The Church that nobody knows will also be the church that focuses upon the whole ministry. It will not say that "our sole purpose is soul winning." No church really understands the New Testament message when it declares its only purpose is evangelism. That is a paramount purpose of the Church. The Great Commission has challenged us to go into all the world and win people to Christ. But having led them to Christ, then what do we do with them? Jesus spent three years training his disciples when they made the commitment to follow him. Paul's epistles were written not to non-Christians but were written to Christians to lead them into a deeper, more mature faith. The church will always say, "Yes, we want to reach people for Christ," but having reached them for Christ, we now have to equip and train them to reach toward "the full maturity of Christ."

One of the reasons we do not have more lay persons in service and ministry is because of the immature level of so many Christians. They have never gotten beyond the entrance into the Christian faith. They are like a newborn child who has never grown beyond the baby level of the Christian faith. The Christian should always be reaching further, growing, developing, maturing, to be more like Christ. The Church that nobody knows will be engaged in the whole ministry which seeks to be evangelistic and bring men and women to Christ, but it will also be concerned about their mind and spirit which has been broken by loneliness, pressures, aches, and pain. The Church that nobody knows will reach out to the total person and provide them counseling and guidance, if they need it. It will minister to them through hospitals, schools, and other agencies, if their needs demand it. This church will be concerned with the total person and not with just an abstract soul. We reach out to the total person by following the example of Christ who ministered to the hurting, lonely, and the needy in society.

A Prophetic Ministry

The Church that nobody knows will also be a church that is a prophetic voice for Christ. It will not be merely an echo of what everybody wants it to say. It will not content itself to reflect the social customs and traditions of its day. The Church that nobody knows will stand up and lift "the mind of Christ" before us and declare that this is what we are to be like. The Church directs us to reach toward maturity. The Church will challenge our prejudices, traditions, customs, mores, and values. It will challenge our materialistic philosophies of life, playboy style of living, apathy, and ingratitude. The church will be a prophetic voice which always seeks to make us more than we are. The true church will never let us turn it into just a comfortable club where we all think alike and act alike. The Church which Jesus established will be a prophetic voice always challenging us to be more than we are.

Martin Luther, the great reformer, wrote to elector George Frederick and declared: "If the conditions that existed in Wittenberg existed in Leipzig, I would go to Leipzig if it rained Duke Georges for nine days, each duke nine times as mad as this one. *He makes my Lord Christ a man of straw!*" The Church that nobody knows will not be a straw church. It will be a church that will dare to be a voice that will challenge the government, schools, and society to follow the mind of Christ in all we do.

A SERVANT CHURCH

The Church that nobody knows will also be a church that is a servant church. It will seek to be like its Lord and lay down its life in service and ministry. It will be willing to go into the world to reach the untouchables, the outcasts, and the needy. It will be willing to give its life to serve in the name of Christ. Its primary concern will not be with saving itself or maintaining itself but in finding ways to serve and minister in the world. The Greek word for deacon is translated servant or bond slave. God's people are engaged in "deaconning" — service. God's people are to be equipped. Why? They are "equipped for work in service." Christians are not equipped to sit, not equipped to be spectators, not equipped to get all our needs satisfied, not equipped simply to enjoy church, but we are equipped to serve — to go into the world to be his people.

When the small struggling Christian church at Antioch received word that the Christians in Jerusalem were living in famine, they didn't whip off a note and say to them: "Gosh, we are really concerned about you. God bless you." They put their money where their concern was. They took up an offering, and the Apostle Paul delivered the money to help meet their needs. The church that is a servant church will always be trying to find avenues to share the gospel with those who are hurting in society.

When Jimmy Allen was pastor of the First Baptist Church in San Antonio, Texas, he talked with one of the doctors in his church and asked him why they had not begun a program to inoculate the people in the city against diphtheria. A tremendous outbreak of diphtheria was imminent. "Well, you know we should have done that, and we talked about it briefly when we had our budget planning committee meeting," the doctor said. "But our budget planning committee meeting took so much time that we did not have time to inoculate the people."

I am not against committee meetings. We have to have them. But we do not want to spend so much time examining ourselves that we refuse to go into the world to reach the hurting, the needy, and the lost. We have to carry the message of Christ to them. The Church that nobody knows will be a church that is always trying "to build up" the fellowship. The image Paul uses here is of stones being properly fitted together. Each Christian makes the church stronger. No Christian tries to downgrade the work of somebody else. He or she is not always criticizing others but will constantly try to build up the church. The Church nobody knows will have room for many thoughts, traditions, and concepts. It will be unwilling to say that there is only one way to look at religious truth. The church needs the voice of the conservative to "conserve" the best in our ancient tradition. But we also need the voice of the liberal who will challenge us to think and see new ways. We will make room for each other, respect each other's opinion, encourage

The Rebirth of the Church

one another, and "speak the truth in love" when we differ with one another.

When one speaks "the truth in love," what a radical difference it makes in our relationship one to the other. But when the truth is spoken selfishly to achieve one's own goal, then the church does not build itself up but destroys itself.

The Church nobody knows will be willing to listen to the voice of Christ and build up and encourage both the conservative and the liberal so that each can find his or her place to minister. Each will be willing not to say that "my way is the only way of seeing Christ" but instead will build each other up, learn from each other, encourage, and support one another.

A UNITED CHURCH

The Church that nobody knows will also be a united church. Paul devoted much of his writing to the problem of divisiveness in the church. Many of his epistles focused on the immaturity of Christians who were so content on getting their own way that they caused strife and division in the church. He encouraged the church to work for unity by reaching toward the "full maturity of Christ." In the fourteenth verse of Ephesians 4, Paul drew upon the image first of an immature child to warn his readers about their behavior. Then he changed his metaphor to a ship that was caught on waves without a rudder. He turned again to another metaphor of dice in a game used by one who misled and cheated his victims. But the mature Christian is founded on Christ, the solid foundation. He or she will "reach toward maturity;" The Church that is built on the foundation of Christ can withstand all kinds of doctrinal differences, because its central creed is "Christ is Lord." The church will continuously labor to be a united church within, and then it will seek to be more united without. I am a Baptist but first I am a Christian. There has to be a dominant commitment to Christ.

Sometimes when I listen to Christians talking about their differences, I wonder if we are not like the blind men examining an elephant. "I've got the trunk and that's the shape of the true church." "I have hold of the trunk." "I have hold of the tail;" "I have the leg." "I have the side." When we emphasize our distinctives, we have difficulty moving closer together and understanding the unity of the Church of Christ. The Church that nobody knows will be a united church.

A military chaplain once spoke about the way soldiers prayed in their foxholes. As he listened to their prayers, he soon learned that it didn't make any difference what denomination or what faith they were. They prayed to God out of their own individual needs. He went on to say that "The Devil displays little terror when he sees a Presbyterian forefinger, or a Baptist middle finger, or an Episcopal thumb, or a Methodist third finger, or some other denominational little finger pointed at him. But when these fingers and that thumb are all doubled up into one compelling fist, then the Devil begins to take notice." I do not believe that our concern should be primarily with our denominational differences, but with ways we can unite under the banner of Christ as Lord and serve him as Church. The Church nobody knows will quit trying to rob each other of members. It will not move into somebody else's neighborhood where somebody else is already ministering but try to work cooperatively together.

The great Baptist Walter Rauschenbusch, after he had finished his article entitled "Why I Am a Baptist," concluded it with these words:

> I should do harm if I gave Baptists the impression that we are the people and there are no others. We are not a perfect denomination. We are capable of being just as narrow and small as anybody. There are fine qualities in which other denominations surpass us. I do not want to foster Baptist self-conceit, because thereby I should grieve the spirit of Christ. I do not want to make Baptists shut themselves up in their little clamshells and be indifferent to the ocean outside of them. I am a Baptist, but I am more than a Baptist. All things are mine. Whether Francis of Assisi, or Luther, or Knox, or Wesley; all

The Rebirth of the Church

are mine because I am Christ's. The old Adam is a strict denominationalist. The new Adam is just a Christian.[10]

The Church nobody knows will be a united church – with its focus on one Lord, one faith based on love and trust, and one baptism. We move toward the goal until "we all attain to the unity of the faith and of the knowledge of the Son of God."

A Pilgrim Church

Then finally the Church nobody knows will be a church that is a pilgrim church. It will realize that God has never called us to stop but always to be in process. The first temple for Israel was a tent — a tabernacle. In its early history Israel was a tent people — people on the move. In the Book of Hebrews, the Christians are described as pilgrims and strangers in the world (Hebrews 11:13). In the small Epistle to Peter the Christians are described as pilgrims (1 Peter 2:11). We are indeed a pilgrim people. We gather in this place to worship, but we scatter into the world knowing that God is never confined to a place. We gather in a church building as a community in fellowship, but we live in the world as God's pilgrim people who must witness, serve, and love in his name. Knowing that God has called us to reach beyond material values, we affirm that no building can be the end of our work for him. We can never place our primary goals in material things, because we are pilgrim people who move through this world to the eternal life which Christ died that we might have.

The Church that nobody knows may be a church that will take forms and shapes that we have never dreamed of before. It may have new ministries and different times of worship. Remember that eleven o'clock was originally picked because it was a convenient time for farmers between milking. There is nothing particularly sacred about that time. The Church nobody knows may select

---

10 Walter Rauschenbusch, "Why I Am a Baptist," Sydnor L. Stealey, editor, A Baptist Treasury (New York: Thomas Y. Crowell Co., 1958), 183-4.

some other hour. We need to be open to the leadership of God to the possibilities before us.

The tearing down of the old Pennsylvania Railroad station while Madison Square Garden was being built is a parable about the church of the future for me. The station was being torn down at the same time they were erecting the Madison Square Garden on that very spot. While they were tearing the train station down, the trains continued to run. They didn't stop a single train. The old train station was slowly dismantled while the new Madison Square Garden was being built, but the trains continued to run during all the changes. I think God's Church that nobody knows will not come into existence just like that, not in a moment or a twinkling of an eye. I think we will keep on serving him while we slowly dismantle the old and the new rises from the old. There will always be some who will have deeper insights into what it is to be like Christ. They will be open and more receptive. Life may move quickly through these church stations, but the Church which Christ is building will continue to rise. We can never contain nor limit Christ with our creeds and systems. He will continue to break the old "wine skins" to bring the freshness and newness of his gospel. My prayer to God is that we will be a congregation and a people that will seek to be a part of the Church that nobody knows. If that is our goal, we will be both relevant and biblical, with roots and fruits. May God grant that we shall have such a vision.

7
THE REBIRTH OF THE CHURCH

Several years ago, I read about two men who lived on a houseboat. They had it securely tied up at a water-front dock. But one night, while they were sleeping, a bad storm arose, and the boat broke its moorings and drifted out to sea. The next morning one of the men woke up and looking outside, ran back in and cried to his friend: "Wake up! Wake up! We're not here anymore!"

There are a lot of people who are saying to the church that "You are not here anymore." There is something radically different about the Church. It is not where it should be as the authentic New Testament Church. Some churches have undergone very drastic changes. I know one church building that has been turned into a beauty shop. Another church building was sold, and the church was made into a warehouse. I have eaten in another church that was sold and turned into a restaurant. Some of you are familiar with a song written by Steve Taylor entitled, "This Disco Used to Be A Cute Cathedral."

> Sell your holy habitats
> that ship's been deserted by sinking rats
> The exclusive place to go
> Is where the pious pogo
> Don't you know
> This disco used to be a cute cathedral
> Where the chosen cha-cha every day of the year

This disco used to be a cute cathedral
Where we only play the stuff you're wanting to hear.[11]

CRITICISM OF THE CHURCH

The Church has changed in a lot of ways over the years. Down through the centuries, many voices said the institutional church is not very close to what the authentic church should be. The philosopher Santayana once said that "the shell of Christendom is broken." "In every age," Gustau Weigel declared, "the institutions (of religion) are dying." But he added, "They never do." Swinburne, the poet, stated that he had great admiration for Christ but despised his "leprous bride" — the Church. Bertrand Russell, the agnostic, once wrote: "I say quite deliberately that the Christian religion as organized in the churches has been and still is the principal enemy of moral progress in the world."

There have been a lot of people who have said to the Church, "You are not here anymore for me. You are not really what you should be." Some New Testament scholars have declared that Jesus never had any intentions of founding an institutional Church. But most believe that Jesus gathered around him a group of disciples which form the nucleus of the Church which he came to begin. The Greek word for church "ecclesia" in Matthew 16:18 is a word which means "the called-out ones" Jesus envisioned the Church not so much as an organization but as an organism — a living group of people — a covenant of believers — a fellowship of disciples. The Church grew out of the group of disciples gathered together in deep commitment to him. But the Church cannot exist merely as an ideal without some kind of institutional form for its habitation. What is needed today is not to do away with all the established churches, but that the churches be reborn again in the image which Christ intended them to be initially. Hans Küng, the noted theologian, has reminded us that "one can only know what the Church

---

11 https://www.elyrics.net/song/s/steve-taylor-lyrics.html.

The Rebirth of the Church

should be now, if one also knows what the Church was originally. This means knowing what the Church of today should be in the light of the Gospel."[12] As followers of Christ, we have to reach back to our original roots and rediscover what the Church really was and should be. When this is done, there will be a rebirth of the Church. In the sixteenth chapter of Matthew three basic ingredients are noted which are essential for the rebirth of the Church. These involve choice, confession, and commission.

A CALL FOR A DECISION

The early disciples faced a choice. They had to decide who Jesus was. At Caesarea Philippi, as recorded in Matthew 16:13-19, Jesus asked them two questions: "Who are people saying that I am?" and "Who do you say that I am?" Look at the place Jesus selected to raise these questions. Caesarea Philippi was renowned for its religious influences. This area was the center for the Syrian worship of Baal. Fourteen temples to Baal had once existed here. Near where Jesus spoke was a deep cavern which some said was the origin of the Greek god of nature, Pan. At one time Caesarea Philippi bore the name of this god. Jesus was speaking to his disciples in the cradle of Greek religion. Close by was the spring which some considered the source of the Jordan River. This river played a central place in the religion of the Jewish nation. Also, nearby was Herod's temple where the godhead of Caesar was enshrined. Surrounded by images of worship from Syria, Greece, Rome, and Judaism, Jesus turned to his disciples and asked them: "Who do people say that I am?" They responded by saying, "Some say that you are John the Baptist — the forerunner of the Messiah. Some say that you are Elijah, the great prophet of miracles and promise. Others say that you are Jeremiah, the prophet of promise and hope."

Then he turned to them and asked, "Who do you say I am?" Silence fell over them. Finally, Peter was the spokesperson. "You are the Christ, the Son of the Living God." Even in their short time

---

12 Hans Küng, *The Church* (New York: Sheed and Ward, 1967), ix.

with him, they had already discovered that the word "man" was not enough to describe him. Prophet, Healer, and Teacher were not enough. During their experience with Jesus, the disciples came to realize that he was the anointed one — the Messiah of God. Later the writers of the New Testament would give him many more titles. There are at least forty-two titles which have been given to Jesus in the New Testament, such as Son of Man, Son of God, Messiah, the Vine, the Good Shepherd, Alpha and Omega, and others. "You are Lord;" they cried.

"Who do men say that I am?" That question has continued to come to persons down through the ages. It comes to you and me. You and I must make the choice. We must decide who this figure Christ is. If there is to be Church, choice continues to confront men and women. Jesus stands at the door of our life and knocks. We have to decide whether we will respond or not.

A Confession of Faith

Hopefully, choice will move on to confession. Peter made a confession of faith in his recognition that Jesus was the Christ. Peter's confession has been a storm-center of the Church down through the ages. Catholics and Protestants have usually been on opposite sides. Some have tried to solve the problem by referring to the Greek language and noting a play on words in the Greek name for Peter and the Greek word for rock which are very similar. This view attempted to place the emphasis on Peter's faith and not on Peter. But Jesus didn't speak Greek, he spoke Aramaic. In Aramaic the word for Peter and rock are the same word.

What was Jesus saying when he stated: "You are Peter and upon you I will build *my* Church?" The Church is built on the confession of Peter. He was the first stone which was built on the foundation stone — Jesus Christ. He was the first to recognize that Jesus Christ was Lord. He became the first stone in the Church. The apostles became the other stones in the foundation of the Church by their confession of faith. All other Christians, through

The Rebirth of the Church

their confessions down through the years have become a part of the foundation of the Church. The Church was built on Peter's confession, the disciple's confession and your confession and mine. The Church was built on each of them and each of us.

Faith cannot be separated from the person who makes it. Peter, in some ways, was the weakest link in the disciples. What irony it seemed to use the phrase rock to describe Peter, because Peter was not rock-like. In his weakness, he denied his Lord. Nevertheless, the Church is built on persons just like Simon Peter. It is built on weak human beings like you and me who commit our lives in trust to him. What does it cost? It cost you your life. It cost you commitment to Christ. It cost the denial of self and committing your life to Jesus Christ as Lord. It is the costliest thing you will ever do. Never forget that! To be Christian, it cost you everything. To commit your life to Christ requires self-denial and taking up your cross to follow in his way.

"The gates of Hades," Jesus said, "will not prevail against his Church." The gates of Hades were a very familiar metaphor to the Jewish people. They were symbolic of the forces of evil and the powers of death. Jesus knew that his disciples would go through misunderstanding, rejection, and persecution. The followers of Jesus Christ have always had to withstand persecutions and rejections. Many have thought they could stamp out the Church. Others have seen the Church as so inept that they thought it could not survive. The Church was seen by many as being so corrupt in the fifteenth century that there seemed to be no possibility for survival. But then, Martin Luther came on the scene, and the Church was reformed. There were many who thought that the Church in England in the nineteenth century was dead, and Wesley began to preach, and the Church was transformed. Many Christians thought that the Church would never be missionary minded again, but then along came William Carey, and there was a rebirth in the Church. God is constantly coming into the life of his people and breathing new life into the Church.

God Continuously Breathes New Life into the Church

When it looks like the Church has been destroyed or is dead, God continues to give it new life. There have always been times when the Church seemed ineffective and impotent. Dorothy Sayers once observed that "the average Church member is about as equipped to do battle on fundamentals with a Marxist atheist as a boy with a peashooter facing a fanfare of machine guns." Today as times in the past, the Church appears weak and inefficient against the forces of evil. Yet Christ continues to work within his Church to strengthen and empower it to meet the powers of darkness. Disciples who have been disciplined and trained will be able to serve Christ more courageously in our modern world.

One night a man approached the minister, Joseph Dowell, after they had heard a magnificent concert by Sir John Barbirolli and the Halle' Orchestra, and asked him: "When are you going to have this place full on a Sunday night?" "I shall have this place full on a Sunday night," he replied, "when like Sir John Barbirolli I have with me eighty trained and disciplined men."

The Church of Jesus Christ will go forward when there are eighty, a hundred, or a thousand men and women who are disciplined, trained, and committed to Jesus Christ as Lord. The Church will make an impact on the world when men and women have confessed their faith and have committed their life to be disciplined and trained by Christ.

Commissioned to Share the Gospel

We are confronted by Christ and have to make a choice, and then following our confession of faith, we are commissioned to go into the world and share the gospel with others. Jesus said to Peter, "I will give to you the keys of the kingdom of heaven." That phrase has caused a lot of misunderstanding in the Church. What is Jesus telling him? He is saying: "You are to be a steward in my kingdom." A steward is someone who manages and administers the affairs of someone else. "The keys to the success of my kingdom's work are in your hands. I will be leaving soon. Peter, you are responsible for sharing my love and grace with others. Whether or not it is successful is in your hands. You are my steward. Carry on my gospel and pass the good news on to others. It is up to you." This seems to be the basic emphasis here.

Now it is up to you and to me to carry the message to others. The "keys to the kingdom" have been passed down through the centuries by others until they have reached you, and now they are in your hands. Have you ever been house hunting and finally came upon a house that you wanted to see? You may have walked up the steps and discovered a sign in the window: "Key next door." You, then, had to go next door to get the key to get in. There are a lot of Christians who want to pass the key next door. But the key is in your hands and in my hands. We are stewards of the Gospel of Christ. We who have received so much are now challenged and commissioned to share this love with other people.

SHARE THE GOOD NEWS OUT OF JOY

I hope that you will share your faith out of a sense of the joy that has come in your life from knowing Jesus Christ as Lord. Jesus said, "I have come that you might have life more abundantly." But he has also come that "your joy might be made full and complete." People should come to Christ because they see within your life and mine an attractiveness that draws them to him. In the small Epistle of Titus, the writer urges the Christians: "Adorn the doctrine of salvation." Let there be an attractiveness about the faith so that people are drawn to Jesus Christ as Lord. The Christian faith is spread most effectively when people are attracted to it. Evil has often been depicted as more attractive than goodness. Satan has disguised himself as an "angel of light." The Church has to labor hard not to let the ways of sin seem more attractive than goodness.

One of the young women in one of my congregations told me about a prayer that one of the deacons in her former church used to pray. It went something like this: "May others come to know you as Lord and Savior through your goodness that they see in us." What a wonderful prayer. May people be drawn to Christ as they see God's goodness in your life and mine. How many people, let me ask you, have you brought to Jesus Christ because you have made the faith attractive? How many of you have led others to Jesus Christ through your demeanor, words, and actions? There should be an attractiveness about our lives that draws people to Christ. Too often critical and negative attitudes turn people away from Christ and his Church. Goodness draws people to Christ.

Several years ago, I saw the play, *To Culebra,* at Actor's Theatre in Louisville, Kentucky, about Ferdinand de Lesseps, who directed the construction of the Suez Canal and, in his later years planned the construction of the Panama Canal. His company went bankrupt trying to dig the canal. One day he was talking to his son about his work, "You must always remember," he said, "that the pessimists are the spectators of life." Many people become discouraged easily and turn away from their goals. Negative and critical attitudes cast discouragement in the paths of others. Anybody can throw obstacles in another's path. What stepping stones do you provide? Anybody can throw obstacles in the way. What helping hands do you extend? When we make the faith attractive, we draw men and women to Christ. A man, who recently joined one of my former churches, said: "I haven't been this excited about a church for years." When we are excited about the faith and our Church's ministry in spreading the gospel, we will share this experience with others.

REKINDLE THE SPIRIT WITHIN

The Church Renewal Committee in one of my churches, which was charged with renewing efforts in our church, adopted the phrase "Rekindle the Spirit Within." What a great phrase! Our prayer is that God will come into our lives and set us aglow with the radiance of God's love, and as his love comes to life within us, hopefully, we will reach out to touch the lives of others with his love, and they in turn will be set on fire for Christ. His love will spread from us to others, and, then from one to another and on and on. "Be aglow with the spirit," Paul reminds the Roman Church (Romans 12:1). Jesus declared, "I came to cast fire upon the earth, and would that it were already kindled" (Luke 12:49). An apathetic and detached attitude cannot be the stance of the Christian. When Christ sets our spirits aflame, we ignite a fire in others. The fire of a burning heart comes from having an experience of the warmth of God's forgiving grace and mercy. His radiant love kindles our love and faith into a glowing zeal for him. The radiance of God's grace has changed us into "a new creation" and this redemptive transition has inspired us to spread the bright flame of God's love into all the world. "I came to cast fire upon the earth," Jesus said, "and would that it were already kindled" (Luke 12:49).

In the First Epistle to Peter 3:8-11, the writer challenges the Christians to *serve Christ with a fervent love*. The Greek word "fervent" may be rendered "tense" from its original meaning. The image is that of an athlete whose muscles are tense or taut in strenuous activity. This Christian love is disciplined and controlled as one equips himself or herself to serve Christ. The intensity of this love challenges each one to reach out to touch others with the power of Christ, even when this love is rejected or misunderstood. This love continues working its power. It is constant and unfailing. This love reaches out to extend itself to its widest dimension. Barriers will not restrain this love. The power of Christ will reach out into the world and transform the lives of others. Love begins with those closest to us, then reaches out to our neighbors and strangers we meet. Then it reaches further into the world to include our enemies. It is an inclusive not exclusive love.

This love will be hospitable, Peter declared further in this epistle. For the first two hundred years, the early Church had no building. Church members had to open their houses to travelling missionaries and other Christians when they were travelling or were persecuted. Love opened its doors to Christians in need, especially in times of persecution. Today the Church's hospitality is a sign of its openness to receive all who are searching to know Christ. Love compels us to share the faith with people wherever we meet them. When a stranger comes in our midst today, we extend our hospitality to include him or her in our community. The stranger is always welcome in the Christian community.

THE SPIRITUAL GIFTS OF ALL CHRISTIANS

Every Christian has some gifts. These gifts, Peter says in this same epistle, are to be used ungrudgingly in the service of Christ. There is no gift so small or too great to be excluded from the practical service of Christ. Our gifts which come to us from God are to be used generously to bring others to know *the* Christ as Lord. As stewards of Christ, we serve in his house — the Church — and acknowledge that all we have and are we owe to him. As good stewards, we share his grace with others. Everything we have is entrusted to us by God to be used in service for him. We offer our gifts to Christ, so his Church can be the agent of reconciliation which he created it to be. The Church is never fully what it should be. We are imperfect. The Church is always in process of being rebuilt. The Church never completes its building process to be like Christ. He comes again and again to breath upon the Church to make it what it should be.

Several years ago, I read a parable about the Church by a man who grew up in central Kentucky named W. W. Grady. His father purchased a sawmill when he was a young boy. To his father's chagrin, he discovered that one of the main bearings had burned out. They tried to locate another one but decided the simplest thing would be to make a new one. They nailed two smooth boards around the main shaft and the housing. They dug around in their scrap metal and found some pieces of babbitt metal. They washed it, cleaned it, and then heated it to remove all the dirt and grit. Then they poured the hot liquid into the mold that they had made for the bearing. After it cooled sufficiently, they bored a hole down through the middle of the bearing. When they bored the hole through it, they discovered that it was not a perfect bearing at all. It had little crevices and other flaws in it. Some thought they should reject this bearing because it was not perfect. But his father said, "No, the flaws and crevices would help lubricate the bearing better." His father turned the steam engine on and the main shaft began to turn. It was not a perfect sawmill. But the huge saw began to sing. The new bearing did its job, and the saw began to cut the wood they needed.

This became a parable for him about the Church. We are brought to Christ as sinners. We come, needing to be washed and cleansed of our sins by the power of his grace. Our sins are burned away by the forgiving grace of his love. Our baptism signifies that we have been cleansed by his love. Then we are put into service for him. We are not perfect instruments. We are flawed and inadequate, but God uses us in his Kingdom's work and his ministry goes on.

From the very beginning of his Church, God has never used perfect instruments. He started with weak Simon Peter, and other ordinary men who were his disciples. The Church continues to be built and rebuilt on persons like you and me as we commit our lives to God. It is always in process of being rebuilt. My prayer is that we will continuously be open to him to let his love flow through us, so his Church might bear his love into the world. May God grant that we will be willing to be one of God's instruments in the world. Will you? It's up to you and me to choose.

8

WHY GO TO CHURCH?

The late C. S. Lewis, who was an agnostic for years before he came to the Christian faith, and later through his writings led many others into a deeper faith, once wrote: "The idea of churchmanship was to me wholly unattractive. I was not in the least anticlerical, but I was deeply anti-ecclesiastical … Though I liked clergymen, as I liked bears, I had little wish to be in the Church as in the zoo. It was; to begin with, a kind of collective; a wearisome 'get-together' affair. I couldn't yet see how a concern of that sort should have anything to do with one's spiritual life."[13] Later Lewis would write about the significance of the church and what it meant. These words, however, reflected where he was for many years.

As a pastor I hear many excuses from people as to why they do not go to church. I could list many reasons people give for not going to church. I want to share a few of these reasons with you and then think with you about why we should go to church. Maybe you will recognize yourself in some of the reasons people give for not going to church.

SOME EXCUSES FOR NOT ATTENDING CHURCH

One of the reasons people give is, "I was *made to go* when I was young." A woman recently said to me: "My mother made me go to church all the time when I was a child. So, I am not going

---

13 C. S. Lewis, *Surprised by Joy* (New York: Harcourt, Brace and Co., 1955), 233-234.

now." She is an elderly woman who is still in a period of teenage rebellion. Her mother also made her eat her food when she was small, made her go to school, made her dress, made her go to bed at night. She didn't give up those habits. Isn't it remarkable how selective we can be in what we decide to give up that our parents made us do when we were small?

Some people do not go to church because they say, "*You have to dress up.*" I have led worship services where the congregation did not dress up at all. I remember the worship services I used to lead in Scout Camp during the summer when I was in college. We would gather for worship down by the lake. Everybody was dressed in Bermuda shorts or very casual clothing. We sang hymns, read Scripture, prayed and I would preach a short sermon. The whole service was very informal and brief. In worship services in resort parks the worshippers, who are traveling and camping, do not dress up. They come as they are to worship. There are many churches today where people do not "dress up" to come to worship.

There are appropriate occasions for not dressing up for worship. But there are times and places where it seems to me that "dressing up" is the right thing to do. If I received an invitation to come to the White House and meet the President, would I go dressed in my blue jeans or Bermuda shorts and tee shirt? I would dress up. The occasion would demand it. Why do many of us dress up when we go to church? We dress up not to impress others with our clothes, but as an acknowledgement of our awareness of the significance of the One in whose presence we come. We dress up to affirm his holiness and greatness. We don't want to come into God's presence in a slip-shod fashion or casual manner. We want to acknowledge the greatness of God.

Others say, "I *need Sunday to rest and be alone.*" We all, of course, need time to rest and be alone. But many persons who use that reason for not going to church on Sunday are often on the golf course or crowded in a stadium watching a ballgame. Rather than spending the time alone, these people are often with throngs of other people busily engaged in activities of all kinds. Sometimes they are so worn out from their "resting" and recreation that they can hardly go back to work on Monday. Little time is actually spent in being still.

Others say, "I need Sunday *to have time for my family.*" They do, of course. But why would you pick the Sunday morning worship hour as the time that you are going to recreate with your family? Many could have leisure time together on Saturday. Why not Sunday afternoon? Would not your family worshipping together to acknowledge the greatest of God and your own need of worship be an appropriate way to spend some time together? "I don't need to go to church," some others declare. "*I have got the electronic church. I can worship by means of television or radio.*" I am not going to say for a moment that T.V. and radio are not significant in helping some people worship. Several of the churches where I was pastor broadcast our morning worship service over the radio. The radio and television serve a ministry to the ill, the homebound, and those who cannot come to church. But ... the electronic church can create a real pseudo-religion for us. It depicts an invisible community and an invisible church with no demands. The electronic church is a church without a support community, without a clear call for Christian responsibility, and without a challenge to authentic discip1eship. Entertainment often becomes its primary focus. "The electronic evangelists," John Killinger notes, "are like water bugs skating on the surface of the pond with little or no acquaintance in ecclesiastical or theological depths." They are unable or unwilling to probe deeply into the faith to give the viewer a religion with deep meaning or sustenance. Instead they often give a shallow concept of what true Christianity is. They have become so obsessed with staying on the air that their primary goal becomes to raise enough money to pay for their programs. The cost is usually in the millions of dollars. Why people continue to support such self-centered consumer religion is beyond me.

Others say. "I'm not going to go to church because *it is always asking for money* and it is always making demands." The church does ask for money, because it telegraphs a clear message which it receives from Jesus Christ: "Where your money is reflects where your heart is." We are not to be just receivers in religion but givers. All you have to do is look at a person's check stubs and you can see what is important in his or her life. The church does make demands upon you financially, but it also calls you to give your time and energy in service. This challenge goes back to our Lord himself who called us to discipleship which requires the committing of one's life to following Christ's way.

I find it interesting that people like to complain about the church asking for money. I used to be on the Board of Directors of the Boy's and Girl's Club in one of the cities where I was pastor. Members of the Board of Directors were asked to contribute a certain amount of money. We were expected to give definite hours of time and service to carry on the programs for these boys and girls. I was a member of a civic club and served on the Board of Directors of that club. Members were required to pay a certain fee to belong to that civic Club, and we were expected to make a stated contribution to support the United Fund. If you didn't pay your dues and make your contributions, you could not be a member. Many of you are members of a country club or have membership in a local gym or health club. You must pay a fee to belong to those organizations, and if you don't pay that fee, you lose your membership. I find it strange that if the church dares to raise a single voice about asking for money to support its ministries, some cry: "How could they possibly do that?"

Others say they don't go to church because, *"they don't get anything out of it."* Many do not get anything out of worship because they have a concept of religion that is "spectators." They view religion primarily as a show, and they sit, watch, and wait to see if it will be entertaining enough. Church worship is seen like a Walmart special. If the service doesn't flash a bright enough light and offer religion at a bargain basement price, they will go to a "church show" that does. Religion is seen primarily as entertainment, and they long for more enticement to feel good. They bring nothing with them to worship and get nothing out of it. A seminary student

The Rebirth of the Church

can sit for weeks or even for years in the library and never read a book and get nothing from the library. A person can walk in an art museum and sit there for hours and get nothing from it, because she has no appreciation for art. Another could listen to Pavarotti sing and feel nothing, because he didn't understand that kind of music or appreciate that magnificent voice. "Church is irrelevant to the lives of many," they say, "because it doesn't give them exactly what they are looking for." Yet they have done nothing to cultivate their "spiritual taste."

Others sometimes say that they don't need the church, because "They are *self-sufficient*." "I am the captain of my own soul. I am the master of my fate. I do not need anybody else," they assert. "I do not want somebody else trying to guide me in understanding God or religion. I can guide my own understanding and discover my own interpretation of religion and life." These people are familiar to us all. Some of them come to a seminary, where they are supposed to be preparing to serve as a minister, with their theology already determined when they enter the door. Reading, lectures by their professors, nobody or anything will change their minds. They already have their understanding of God, the Scriptures, and the Christian life and declare: "Don't try to teach me anything different!" What kind of medical doctor would a person make who on entering medical school to begin learning how to be a doctor declared: "I already know everything I need to know about medicine." He or she would flunk out, hopefully, in a week! No one could become a doctor, a lawyer, or engineer without the willingness to expose himself or herself to the growth necessary to learn that profession. These persons sometimes attend church but are unwilling to open their minds and grow deeper in the faith. Their mind is closed, and they refuse to be responsive to new insights or possibilities other than their own.

Sometimes people say they don't go to church, because there are *hypocrites in the church*. I want to tell you very honestly; I have never known many hypocrites in the church. A hypocrite is a person who is play acting, who wears a mask pretending to be something that he or she is not. Intention is the main factor here. A hypocrite has no intention of trying to be like Christ. A hypocrite is not somebody who wants to be like Christ and fails. A hypocrite is somebody who does not intend to try to be like Christ. The church is indeed filled up with a lot of people who are not like Christ. They are far from realizing his high standards. But they are not hypocritical. They are really trying to be more like Christ. They fail, still sin, but they keep on reaching. I have never heard many people say, "I am going to quit going to medical doctors because I heard of one who was a quack." But some quit going to church because they heard about a preacher who ran off with somebody's wife in the church, or they heard about some preacher who stole some church funds. They have given up on church. One bad apple doesn't mean that the whole church is full of hypocrites. Don't let weak Christians or even hypocrites keep you from worshipping God.

Reasons for Attending Church

There are many reasons people don't go to church. The ones we have alluded to may be yours sometimes. Many others could be noted. In an article published in The Christian Century, "I don't go to church," Adam J. Copeland, a professor at Luther Seminary in St. Paul, Minnesota, list reasons why he and his wife have stopped attending church. He acknowledges that they don't need a church to be perfect, but just to be "enough" community, worship, and seeking of truth. "I still have hope in the power of the Christian community," Copeland concludes, "even after all the difficult church visits."[14] I have not given up on the church and, therefore, I want to put the primary focus on why we should go to church. Let us turn now to these reasons. I know some people who go to church because it is simply part of their family heritage. They go today because their parents brought them when they were young. Others go because their friends are there, or because the church is friendly, or it has good programs for children, youth, or adults.

---

14 Adam J. Copeland, "Why I don't go to church," The Christian Century (March 27, 2019), 11.

The Rebirth of the Church

Others like the preacher or the music. These reasons for going to church are not wrong. We all want a church that offers a variety of programs and meets needs in our life, but our reasons for going to church should be much deeper and on a more profound level than these kinds of surface reasons that we often select. I offer to you the following suggestions.

Provides an Oasis Where We Can Worship God

First, we should go to church because it is the place that is set aside to worship God. It is the place built where we can gather together as a community of faith and declare as Isaiah did: "Holy, holy, holy is the Lord God of hosts." This church and other churches are built to acknowledge the reality of the living God who is beyond us. We say with the Westminster Confession that "the chief end of man is to glorify God and to enjoy him forever." We come to church to glorify him and to attest to his reality. The word worship means "worth ship." We worship because we ascribe great worth to God. He is the One worthy of our worship. We come to adore him, pray to him, and to kneel in thanksgiving before his awesome presence. His higher worth forces us to get our priorities in order. Worship acknowledges that the material world is not all there is to reality. The spiritual world is real, and we bow before the Creator of all of life.

We gather together in worship acknowledging that there is a need beyond ourselves which we cannot satisfy in and of ourselves. The need for spiritual help beyond ourselves is reflected all through our society today even by those who claim to be non-religious. Why do so many people read horoscopes? Why do people buy Ouija boards? Why is there so much interest in Eastern religions, especially Zen Buddhism? Why is there so much interest in spiritualism? All this interest attests to the fact that there is an awareness on the part of many that there is a spiritual force beyond themselves which they long to know. We gather in worship to acknowledge the reality of that God.

You may have walked through your yard or by a house that has been abandoned and come across a board lying in the grass. When you kicked the board over, did you notice what the vegetation underneath that board looked like when the board had been lying there for a long time? The vegetation under the board had turned white and become distorted. If the board is there long enough, it will kill the vegetation. Why does the vegetation look like that? It has been cut off from the sunlight — its source of life. Our lives, when they are cut off from worship, become distorted and lose their true color. We lose contact with the source for high standards and values. We become empty and distorted, because we are cut off from the very source of our being itself — God.

Worship is not to be a momentary, occasional affair. To be vital, worship is ongoing and continuous. The need to worship is built into our very being itself. One of the ten commandments reminds us "To remember the Sabbath day to keep it holy." When one does not come apart for worship, there is something that dries up within us and deadness begins to consume our life. We read in the New Testament "that Jesus went to the synagogue as his custom was." He had a habit of going to church week after week. He didn't go there just because he enjoyed the preaching, or he enjoyed the people, or they were friendly to him, or they were nice to him when he was a boy. It was "his custom" to go. Out of his own deep need for reverence, he weekly offered worship to his Father. Within each of us, there is a "plant" called reverence which needs watering weekly. We come to church because there is a deep need to worship God.

A Place for Fellowship

The second reason I go to church is because of fellowship. Fellowship is experienced on many levels. There is local fellowship. Where there is real fellowship, there will be friendship. Fellowship and friendship cannot be equated. But there is really nothing much worse than a church that is unfriendly, where people never speak to each other. A man went to worship in a church once during the summertime. He saw the advertisement on their bulletin board which read, "It's cool inside." When he walked out of the church, he went over to the board and wrote underneath these words: "Brother, you said it!" He wasn't speaking just about the temperature inside either, but about the way the people responded to him. He found no sense of interest or concern for him.

William Willimon told about a man who had been visiting his church and he had contacted him in hope that he would join. After he missed a couple of Sundays, he called him to ask if he had made a decision. "In the beginning I really liked your church," the man responded. "I liked the worship services, and I enjoyed visiting in the church school classes. But frankly — I don't mean this as a criticism — the better I got to know your people, the more I disliked them."

What an indictment of the church. What did he discover? In many churches these people are negative and constantly complaining. Nothing suits them. There is no joy in being around them. Where Christ is present in his church, there should be a real fellowship that expresses love, graciousness, and encouragement. A positive message is received that "Friends are here!" There is a real sense of family where one finds care and support in times of need.

But real fellowship reaches beyond the local level. When you and I are in the fellowship of Christ, we are aware that it is a spiritual fellowship. Christian fellowship is not just getting together for meals and having socials, but it is a spiritual community where Christ himself is Lord. The presence of Christ sustains the church. This is what the writer of the Book of Hebrews is talking about. He described the fellowship which Jesus Christ himself founded as "the church of the firstborn" (Hebrews 12:22-25). Christ is Lord. The key ingredient in any church's fellowship is the confession by each believer that Christ is Lord.

But the church is also *a universal fellowship*. We join hands with other Christians who down through the ages have committed their lives in faith to Christ. You and I are part not only of a local fellowship but are linked to the universal church — the church, which was founded by Christ where Peter, Mary Magdalene. Paul, Phoebe, Augustine, Luther, Calvin, Wesley, Lottie Moon, Annie Armstrong, Albert Schweitzer, and countless numbers have pledged their allegiance to Jesus Christ. Thousands of people in Africa, Russia, China, Japan, Europe and around the world are bound together in this universal church. Yes, the church is local but also timeless, international, interracial, and universal. I want to be a part of that kind of church.

I love to have a fire on a cold winter night. But one thing I learned a long time ago about fires is that if one of the logs falls away from the others, it soon begins to cool and loses it glow and warmth. That log has to be brought back in close to the others if it is to continue burning and generate heat. If one is separated from the warmth of the Christian fellowship, that life grows cool and lifeless. The fellowship sustains us.

The writer to Hebrews writes about "the sprinkling of blood" (Hebrews 12: 23) which reminds us that the church was founded on the death of Jesus Christ. He laid down his life for his church. It is a redeemed fellowship. The church is never *my* church nor your church. It is Christ's church. It was Christ who died for his church. The church is a redeemed fellowship — a community committed to Christ. Where two or three are gathered together, he is in their midst. I come to this place, so I can be in that kind of fellowship.

THE CHURCH PROVIDES AN OPPORTUNITY TO EXPERIENCE GOD'S GRACE

My third reason for going to church is because the church is the medium that dispenses and shares the grace of God. Where else can you go to understand and find out about the grace of God other than the church? The church is the institution that carries the message of God forward. It is the institution that shares the good news of God with others. In church we are made aware of our own sinfulness, God's love, and salvation.

The Rebirth of the Church

I am proud of the church, proud of its tradition. Down through the centuries it has been the agency — the medium — which has established schools, hospitals, children's homes, and great universities like Princeton and Harvard. They came out of the church's mission. I am proud of that kind of tradition. I know what the church has done for good through the centuries. I know of no one who wants to live in a community where there are no churches. Church always makes a difference for good in a community. I am proud of the church and its rich tradition.

Through the church I first discovered God. As a child my parents brought me to church, and it was there I learned of God's grace and his redeeming power. It was there I first learned about the mission and ministry of the church. I am proud to perpetuate God's love through his institutional church. God's grace offers people a second chance, an opportunity to begin again.

I remember a man in my first congregation who looked like one of the roughest persons I had ever seen in my life. I was told that Johnny wasn't a Christian. I was asked as a very young minister if I would go by and talk with him. To be honest with you I felt very uncomfortable around Johnny. He was a great big old gruff looking guy and I wasn't sure what he might say or do. But I went by and talked to Johnny one day. I spoke to him about his need to give his life to Christ. Surprisingly, to this young preacher he did. He committed his life to Christ, made a confession of faith in church, was baptized, and continued to come regularly to church. Years later, when I went back to preach in that little country church, Johnny was sitting in the pews with his family. He had made a commitment of his life to Christ, and he learned about that grace in church.

I received a telephone call from a young woman several years ago in one of my churches. She said she wanted to come and talk to me about the church. She had been listening to our services on the radio. She came by and indicated that she was not a Christian, but wanted to become one. We talked about the saving grace of Christ, and she gave her heart to him. The next Sunday she made her confession of faith and united with our church and has continued to be a faithful part of that community. A young teenager invited a friend who had not gone to church much in his life. He came to our church and learned about Christ, made a confession of faith, and continued to be a vital part of our youth group. These persons discovered Christ through his church where God's grace is dispensed. I come to church to be a part of the continuing work of Christ in the world.

A Vision for Life's Meaning

My fourth reason for coming to church is because it is here that a vision is lifted before us of what life can be like. I do not have to be crushed by sin, burdened by mediocrity, or live on the lowest plains. God calls us to the highest and best we can be. He calls us to climb our spiritual Mount Zion. He calls us to the top of Calvary and to measure our lives by the stature of Christ, to look at the possibilities of what we can be like as we commit our lives to Christ. He lifts our horizons to the highest and best. We can never be content to be our own judges, measure our own worth and values, but strive to reach for the standards which Christ lifts before us. As Isaiah had a vision of the Lord high and lifted up, we look upward to God for his vision of what we can be as we are challenged to reach higher. We are continuously being remade by forces that influence our lives. I come to church, so I might be enriched by the presence of Christ, his teachings, the church's rich tradition, and the constant challenge held before me to reach higher to be like our Lord.

Receive Strength for Life's Journey

Then finally I come to church because it is the place that gives me strength to face life's difficulties and tragedies. The church offers us hope in our brokenness. It offers us direction for our meaninglessness. It offers us support in our times of grief, depression, loneliness, and stress. It offers us friends who gather around to sup-

The Rebirth of the Church

port us in times of divorce, friends who encourage us and sustain us in times of sickness, pain, and grief. It offers us a community of fellowship that sustains us. It provides us a family that encircles us with its love and support.

When our nation went through the tragic loss of six astronauts and a young school teacher in the explosion of our space shuttle several years ago, our people came together in mourning. I didn't hear people saying: "Let me go off and be by myself." There was a call for togetherness. A time of national grief was proclaimed. We were asked to turn on our automobile headlights to indicate our common sorrow in this tragedy. We drew strength from each other. The church brings us together, so we can find strength from each other and the presence of God to face the tragedies, burdens and hurts of life which we have insufficient strength to bear by ourselves. I have always found it sad to hold a funeral service for a family that has no church tradition, no church support group, because they have drifted away from the church or have never been a member of a church. In the time of greatest need, they have cut themselves off from their strongest support group — the church.

Leo Tolstoy came to a very difficult time in his life, and even contemplated suicide. He used to hide rope because he was afraid he might hang himself. But he found hope in the words that he had learned at church: "The eternal God is my refuge." Even in his darkest of days those words gave him strength to go on. Bit by bit he found his way back. These words of hope guided him back to inner peace and composure. I come to church because it is the place in society which offers me strength, encouragement and support. No other institution can ever really do that.

As you are reading this, if you are not attending church now, or even if you are attending on a regular basis, I want to challenge you to join the church again. Join it again in your commitment to be more faithful in your worship. Join it again in seeking to be open to the leadership of God. Join it again in being more responsive to the high vision which God is calling you to be like. Recommit yourself to be a part of the authentic fellowship of Christ which seeks to support and undergird one another. Be willing to lean upon the church in your times of need. Covenant together now in a silent commitment that you will walk more closely with Christ and work more faithfully through his church. I hope this day that you will make a silent prayer to love your church more and to serve God better through it. Remember Christ died for his Church. We ought to be willing to live for it.

9
THE MINISTRY OF THE CHURCH

Suppose when you came to church on the next Sunday morning there was a sign posted on every door which read, "Building for Rent or For Sale, Church Going Out of Business." Suppose that sign was not only nailed to your door but to the door of every church in your city and around the world. The church is for sale or rent and is going out of business for lack of interest, lack of support, and lack of involvement.

THE DECLINE OF TODAY'S CHURCHES

Karl Heim, a German theologian, once used another image about the Church. He compared the Church to a ship. On the deck of the ship many festivities and beautiful music are heard. But below the water line there is a huge hole in the ship, and though the pumps are manned night and day, the ship is sinking hourly. There are some today who are not making very positive statements about the future of the Church. Look at what is happening to many of the churches today. Baptists, one of the most evangelical of all denominations, have slipped in baptisms, and several of their churches are closing or being sold. The Methodist, Lutheran, Episcopal churches have an overall decline in membership and so have most other denominations. A part of the problem may be too much emphasis on denominational distinctives and inter-denominational differences and not enough emphasis on genuine concern for ministry.

Too many people today want what I would call "consumer religion." They just want religion to be like everything else in life.

Consumers buy a product if they like it, and, if they don't, then they won't purchase it. Consumers in religion shop around to find what seems to fit best for them. They reject a church if it does not meet their needs. They just shop around until they find what satisfies them. Religion is just a consumer product like everything else to them.

Others suffer from what I call "hocus pocus, mumbo jumbo religion." These people want instant results from religion without any responsibility, obligation, commitment, cost, and without really believing anything. There are others who want a "sphinx" religion. Like the grand monument of the centuries, they remain "sphinx"-like silent and uninvolved with the history which is happening all around them. They don't really do anything.

We have to be careful that we do not equate form with force. We cannot identify attending church with being church. We cannot identify being at church with being right with God. The Church will not survive unless it discovers its basic ministry. Often it has forsaken it and identified completely with the world. Sometimes one cannot tell the difference between the Church and other organizations in the world. T. W. Manson, a noted New Testament scholar, once wrote, "There is only one essential ministry in the church, the perpetual ministry of the risen and ever-present Lord himself."[15] Our ministry is to be the ministry of Christ — to perpetuate what he started in the world. The Church's ministry is derived from and dependent upon its Lord. Let's see if we can rediscover what that ministry is.

A Ministry of Reconciliation

One of the clear thrusts of our Lord's ministry is that it was a ministry of reconciliation. Jesus said, "I have come to seek and to save that which is lost." We have a world filled with all kinds of lostness and brokenness. Men and women are estranged from God. They are fragmented in their relationship with one another and

---

15 T. W. Manson, *The Church's Ministry* (Philadelphia: The Westminster Press, 1948), 107.

The Rebirth of the Church

do not understand their authentic personhood. Jesus told various parables to describe different ways individuals could be lost. He told a parable about a lost sheep that wandered off from the rest of the flock. Sometimes *the lostness we experience can be aimlessness, purposelessness, meaninglessness, or life without direction or guidance.* Many are busy going without knowing where they are going. Some of us are lost like the parable about the woman who dropped some coins and could not find them. This lostness seems to be *the result of carelessness.* We feel that we are the victims of circumstances and whatever has happened is not really our fault. Environmental factors have created our situations and we are simply caught in the web of life. We have been influenced by our friends, schoolmates, family, and others. We were caught by these circumstances and were pulled down the paths of sin.

Others are lost like the Prodigal Son whom Jesus described in a parable. Our *lostness is our own making.* We set our own direction. We have rebelled. We have wanted our goods, our way, and have turned away from the Father and gone to a far country to waste our life in riotous living. There are others though who have a lostness like the elder brother. But they are still lost. They are *lost in self-righteousness and respectability.* They see themselves as superior to other persons and remain unaware that they are still lost, cut off, and fragmented from God.

Three times in Paul's Second Epistle to the Corinthian Church (5:18-28) he writes about men and women being reconciled to God. It was not God who needed to be reconciled to us. We are the ones who needed to repent and surrender to God's love. Sin had not made God angry with humanity and made God stop loving us. We, as men and women, had erected the barrier between us and God, and we are the ones who need to come back to the God who loves us. The root idea of the word reconciliation is change. Reconciliation is a changed relationship. A relationship by humanity which was broken and fragmented with God has been restored. Reconciliation has provided us with a new relationship with God.

On one of Dr. Howard Thurman's trips to India, the noted minister and his wife had gone to bed when they heard a knock at the door. Dr. Thurman got up and went to the door and saw a young dark-skinned boy standing there. He could tell by his clothes that he was an untouchable. The young boy spoke in good English and said, "Sahib Doctor, I stood outside the building and listened to your lecture. Tell me, please, can you give some hope to a nobody?"

The good news of the gospel is yes there is hope for the hopeless. For those who feel broken and fragmented, Christ has come to give us life. The cross of Christ is the supreme revelation of God's love for us. In the cross we see how deep God's love is. He has come to restore broken relationships and set us right with God. Now we in the church have been given the ministry of reconciliation. As our Lord himself came to bring people into a right relationship with God, now the church's ministry is to go into the world and share the news that broken people can find restoration, that those who are fragmented can find healing, those who are broken can find wholeness in what Christ can do for them. You and I must carry that message to them.

Proclaiming Our Gospel

In Romans 2:16, Paul uses a phrase that causes some people to flinch. He writes about "my gospel." We want to say, "Just a minute, Paul. Isn't it always 'the' gospel?" Yes, it is "the" gospel, but unless it is "your" gospel and "my" gospel, is it ever really the gospel to us? Jesus Christ was the incarnate One who revealed to us what God was like. The Church is the continuous incarnation. The Eternal Word has to have some fleshly form. The word that has come into our life and changes us has to be translated so that the world can see that God is still among us.

When you talk to people and ask them how they became a Christian, almost always they tell you about a particular person who brought them to Christ. It may have been a mother, father, brother, sister, friend, or Sunday-School teacher — but almost always they point to another person who shared his or her gospel with them. We have been given the ministry of reconciliation. The other night someone asked a new church member how he started coming to our church. "The answer," he said, "is very simple. Somebody invited me." People come to Christ because others like you share the good news with them. We have been given the ministry of reconciliation, so others can know the love of Christ.

A SERVANT MINISTRY

Go with me further and see that one of the essential ministries of Christ was the servant ministry. Jesus identified himself with the image of the Suffering Servant from Isaiah. He said, "I came not to be ministered unto, but to minister and to give my life a ransom for many." "If anyone would be first, he must be last of all." "The greatest of all is the servant of all" (Mark 10:44). Jesus took a towel and a basin and girded himself and washed the feet of his disciples. He indicated to them by this act what kind of ministry they should take — a servant ministry. Jesus said, "I have given you an example that you should do unto others as I have done unto you." His ministry was to be servant. The Church's ministry is to take the form of a servant in the world. The Church is not to be served or to serve us, but to minister in the world in Christ's name.

What does it mean to be a servant? In a parable recorded in Luke 17, Jesus spoke about a man who was a servant. He returned home, after working in the fields and did the bidding of his master. He cooked a meal, met all the needs of the master, and then took care of his own needs. Four basic points can quickly be drawn from this parable about a servant. I am indebted to Leonard Griffith for these suggestions.[16] A servant is one who works in somebody else's house. It is not your own but somebody else's. A servant is someone who meets somebody else's needs. A servant is one who works at somebody else's convenience. A servant is one who works

---
16 Leonard Griffith, *We Have This Ministry* (Waco: Word Books, 1973), 50-58

without being thanked. We have really missed understanding what Church is when we overlook these four characteristics. We work in our master's house. We serve to meet the needs of others in society and not for what we can get from it. We work at the convenience of others. When a need becomes apparent, we respond. We do not minister only when we want to, and when it is the right time for us, but at the needs of others. We are at their disposal. We serve even if people never say, "Thank you." "I appreciate your doing it." "You are gracious."

Let me share some of the servant ministries from one of the churches where I was pastor, St. Matthews Baptist Church in Louisville, Kentucky. Some of these ministries came about through the visions of one of our own lay persons. While I was there, one of our members received a special citation for his work in our Nursing Home Ministry. Mr. Clyde Carroll, who founded our Nursing Home Ministry, was honored for his work. Our Nursing Home Ministry began with the vision of one lay person and that service was active in seventeen nursing homes with a hundred people serving weekly. They got nothing from it other than the joy of helping others. Our church had a HUGG Ministry in which we went into the homes of our church people, who were unable to come to church, and ministered to their needs. Our church had a Job Club which helped people find a job when they did not have one. We established the Wayne Oates Counseling Center in our church where people could come and find help in times of need. We had Widow and Widower Support groups and divorce support groups. Income Tax preparation for the elderly was also provided. We had a clothing closet. We had an Alzheimer's Day Care Center which gave an adult respite program for persons with Alzheimer's disease. We had a Kindergarten, Nursery School, and a Mother's Day Out program.

Programs of all kind reached out to the aging and needy. The opportunities for service in our churches are endless. The ministries for service arise as you and I see them and respond to meet them. A program came about in our church's ministry to the Spanish

The Rebirth of the Church

speaking people in our community. There was a need, and we had the resources and we reached out to meet it. We cannot seek just what can be done for us, but we are challenged to see what we can do in the name of Christ to minister and serve.

You may have seen the cartoon recently. The pilot of the plane comes back to speak to the passengers. They could tell that the plane was in trouble. He has a parachute on and turns and looks back at the passengers and says, "Remain calm. I'm going for help."

WE ARE CALLED TO RESPOND

When some people get in a crisis, their response is to run from it. However, Christ has called us to involvement. The ministry of the Church is not to be the work of the clergy alone. The Church is not made up of a Society of Spectators or an Association of Onlookers. The Church is not made up of an Uninvolved Critic Society, nor can it be composed of "You Do It and I'll Sit Back and Complain Club." The Church is called to be involved in the needs of humanity, Every Christian is responsible for service, because you are a minister. The call to serve is not just for the clergy, but all lay persons are commissioned for ministry. When you were called to salvation, you were called to ministry. If you have been redeemed by Christ, then you have been called to ministry. There is NO exception. Every single one of us has been called to a ministry of reconciliation and servant ministry for Christ in the world.

In the Book of Hebrews (5:12) the writer addressed the Christians with the directive: "By this time some of *you* should be teachers." I always have to smile a bit when people complain that the church does not have enough Sunday-School teachers and they themselves are never willing to give any time to teach. They sometimes complain about people who serve on committees. "They always use the same people;" they say. But when they are asked, they are unwilling to accept any responsibility. You have no choice, if you have been converted by Christ, you have been called to ministry, or you have not been converted. There is no exception.

There are tasks we need to do in every church building. There are ministries which are absolutely essential to care for the building and its programs, but the real ministry of the church does not take place in this building. This building is the base of operation, the headquarters to prepare us to go into the world and minister through your job, through your recreation, and through everything you do to be Church in the world.

Several years ago, I heard Bill Jones, a pastor then in New York City, speak. Being a city boy, he said that it was quite an experience for him to go visit his grandfather on his farm. It seemed like the middle of the night when his grandfather got him up. He said the sun wasn't even up and yet they were out feeding the chickens and pigs, milking the cows and doing all the necessary tasks. Finally, he got to eat breakfast at six o'clock. It seemed he had been working all day, and he was exhausted. He looked over at his grandfather while they were eating breakfast and said: "Gee, granddaddy, I'm tired. We have really been working hard." His grandfather looked back at him, laughed and said, "Son, you don't understand. We have just been doing the chores. The real work is out in the field. We are leaving in just a moment to do the real work."

All our work in our building is essential and important, but it is really just the necessary chores. The real ministry is in the world. And YOU and I are ministers in the world or we do not know Christ. We are all his people. The word laity means "belonging to the people." The ministry of Christ in the world is your ministry and my ministry. It belongs to all the people of God.

An Equipping Ministry

Would you not agree with me that the ministry of the church is also an equipping ministry? We can do our best ministry when we are trained most effectively to do it. The Danish theologian Søren Kierkegaard tells about a circus that came to the outskirts of a small Danish town and set up its tent. The big tent caught fire right before the evening show was to begin. A circus clown was

The Rebirth of the Church

sent to the town to tell the people that the circus tent was on fire and to bring help. The clown came running into town and told the people what had happened, but they laughed at him. Clowns are paid to be funny. Clowns are supposed to make you laugh and entertain you. They thought that this was a gimmick to get people to come and see the show. They did not realize until it was too late that there was a real fire.

I don't want you to press this analogy too far, but ministers are like clowns. We are the religious clowns. We are paid professional people who do religious work. When I talk to somebody about Christ, people expect that. That is seen as a part of my job. But, when you as a lay person do it, it is perceived differently. The real ministry of the Church will be done by lay-Christians who serve in the world. Christ is seen through all your life. The professional ministers are called primarily to train lay persons for their ministry. The pastor and other ministerial staff have a responsibility to be equippers, enablers, facilitators preparing others to serve Christ more effectively in the world.

In one of my churches we were very fortunate to have the Dean of the School of Theology from Southern Seminary as well as the Dean of Church Music in our congregation. Neither one of these Deans could do all the work in their particular schools. They are well trained and are specialists in several areas. But Dr. Price could not do all the teaching of music in the Music School, and Dr. Bennett couldn't do all the teaching of theology in the School of Theology. They worked with other professors, each using his or her gifts and training in a specialized area of concentration. They trained and equipped others to minister more effectively.

No pastor can do all the work in a church. As pastor and clergy, we seek to train and equip others to do the work of ministry. We work beside you but cannot do all the work. When both the clergy and laity understand their ministry more effectively, the Church will be revolutionized. Can you imagine what would really happen if every Christian really understood that he or she is a minister!

Our churches would be revolutionized. Every church would be radically changed.

Did you hear about the woman in a nursing home in Macon, Georgia who sent her engagement ring to the Home Mission Board? She indicated that she wanted it to be used "for some young missions' women or to best advantage." The employees of the Mission Board were so moved by this gesture that they bought the ring, gave the money to missions, and enshrined the ring as a reminder of the sacrifice and devotion to missions of Myla Guard. When Mrs. Guard died, her funeral had a mission emphasis. "I am perfectly sure," her daughter said, "that she is at this moment looking down from heaven, wondering why those slow church people don't do more for the cause of missions."

You and I need to recapture our sense of responsibility that every Christian is called to minister. Every Christian has the responsibility of sharing the good news of Jesus Christ with others. No one believes that a medical student is supposed to spend his or her life merely listening to lectures about medicine. At some point a doctor has to practice the healing he or she has been trained to do. So, the Christian cannot be satisfied simply to listen to the gospel message. Every Christian is charged with sharing this good news with others. We must go!

About a month after President John Kennedy was assassinated, a memorial service was held at Arlington National Cemetery. Following the service, someone lit a candle from the flame on his grave. That candle lit another and another and another. In the darkness of that December night one could see thousands of candles being carried across the bridges and scattering into Washington and parts of Virginia. Everywhere they went in the darkness of that night, the flames from those candles cast their light.

We gather together in this building as church to ignite our flame for Christ and keep its glow burning. We then leave this place and scatter into the world to let our light shine for Christ to point others to the Light so they, too, can come to know Christ as Lord. The ministry of the Church is the ministry of reconciliation. It is a servant ministry. It is an equipping ministry. You and I are called to perpetuate the ministry of Christ. I hope and pray that you will capture a glimpse of what God expects you to do as his minister.

10

Addressing the Gospel to Young Adults: Is God Over Thirty?

He was so young — too young by almost any standard. "Where did he get such authority to teach as he did?" the religious leaders asked. He had not been to any theological schools. No one knew of any special teachers under whom he had sat and studied. He began his ministry at thirty. In a few short months, maybe a few years, it was over. This Jesus from Nazareth was placed on a cross and cried: "It is finished." He died at only thirty-three. He was a young man.

Down through the ages, there has been a continuous struggle between the youth and the elderly about who has the deeper insights into life. One side or the other has tended to reject the other. You may have heard this little ditty.

> Said Adam to Eve,
> "I begin to perceive
> That even young Abel
> Whom we raised is unstable:
> And now it is plain
> We shall have to raise Cain."

Today's young adults did not invent the "generation gap." The scriptures reveal this ongoing conflict. Is it not possible that the struggle between David, who later became the King of Israel, and King Saul was because the older Saul saw the younger David as a threat to him? Who knows? I believe that the generation conflict was certainly a part of their clash when Saul heard songs that said, "Saul has slain his thousands but David his tens of thousands." The conflict between the generations has been around for a long time.

It wasn't too long ago that many of the young adults in our country had a phrase that was very popular. "Don't trust anybody over thirty!" they cried. I think there are many young people today who still feel that way. Of all the areas where young adults seem to be unwilling to trust anybody over thirty today, the institutional church is at the top of the list. The church is seen as an old institution. The church is at least two thousand years old. A congregation in the United States may happen to have a new building, but in many parts of our country, and especially in Europe, church buildings are indeed ancient. Many of them are centuries old. The book we study called the Bible is thousands of years old. Many of the creeds and the doctrinal systems of the church are ancient. Even God is often depicted as an old man with a long beard, living off yonder in space. Young adults ask, "How can you possibly trust any kind of institution that is as old as the church? You can only trust someone or something that is young."

DON'T TRUST THE INSTITUTIONAL CHURCH

Well, what are some of the young adults saying to the church today? For one thing, they are saying they don't trust the institutional church. But this distrust is not limited just to the very young. This distrust extends all the way up to the millennials and sometimes beyond. The young adults no longer trust the institutions of religion. They see them as crumbling structures, and they are not sure they will survive. Their distrust of institutional religion, however, doesn't mean that they are not interested in Jesus. This doesn't mean they are not interested in religion. Their distrust is directed against the institutions of religion.

On many college and university campuses today, the most popular courses other than ones on some form of sexuality are often courses on religion. When a student was asked why he was taking a religion course, he responded: "It is the only course on this campus that deals with ultimate questions. It is the only course that is struggling with what gives meaning to my life."

In one of the communities where I was pastor, I taught a course in a local college entitled "The Search for Meaning." College students came to that class who had never read a single book in the Bible. The biblical book that we read in that class was Job. And it was the first time most of them had ever encountered a book in the Bible. But they devoured it when they realized it focused on the question about whether life had any meaning. They discovered that the Bible was dealing with ultimate questions. Many students in college are still interested in the Old Testament prophets, because of the prophets' concern for justice and righteousness. Students are still interested in reading the teachings of Jesus and some of the writings of Paul. They will read books by people like Kierkegaard, Bonhoeffer, Martin Luther King, Jr., and Mother Teresa, because these people stimulate and challenge them to think about life and ultimate questions. But the institutional church ... That isn't something they care much about at all.

I also wonder sometimes if the institutional church will survive. I don't know. They may not survive in the forms that we know today. They may not even exist today in the way that God wants them to survive in the future. I am certainly not a prophet, but I think if the church **is** going to survive and minister to the youth in the years to come it must have several ingredients. Let me mention several of these to you.

A CENTER FOR WORSHIP

First, it will have to be *a center for worship*. It must be a place where youth as well as adults will want to come to worship. That may mean that we will have to have various forms of worship services. Some of these services may even meet at different times, maybe even on a day other than Sunday. Some of these services may take a shape and form that is radically different from what worship is like today. Who knows? Worship is the most important thing the church does, and we can't begin to imagine the shapes and forms it may take in the future. We have to be open to the moving of God in whatever way God chooses to move.

A Center for Learning

Secondly, if young people are going to be drawn to the church, it will also need to be *a center for learning*. I like the phrase that Elton Trueblood used one time when he urged the church to be a mini-theological seminary. The church needs to be a place where those of us who have really met Jesus Christ attempt to teach and educate ourselves and others in the Christian faith. This learning center will be a place where we read books and watch videos or listen to audio presentations and draw on other resources that will nurture, edify, and help us grow as Christians. I do not believe Christians can grow effectively without reading. Our churches need to have solid theological libraries where people can be exposed to the great biblical scholars and theologians. We don't learn about the Bible or God by osmosis. We must read the Bible, study it, and dig into it.

Our beliefs will become incarnational as we see them reflected in the lives of other Christian people. What we believe will be seen in how we live and act every day. Our faith will not be confined to books, but every Christian will become a "living epistle" to others. It is essential for the church to be a learning center.

A Center for Healing

Thirdly, the church needs to be *a center for healing*. The church needs to become a hospital, if you please. It will be a healing center for those who are sinners, a place where the healing grace of God is experienced. It needs to be a place of healing where persons come under the dimension of God's love and they experience forgiveness. Having experienced the initial grace of God, the church continues

The Rebirth of the Church

to be a healing center for whatever it is that tears a person's life apart. In the church a person can find wholeness, completeness as one comes to God.

The church should seek to do more than touch superficial issues and trivialities. The church needs to dig down to the source of the problems and seek to bring healing there. It will not bring real healing if it deals only with surface matters or pretends something has happened when it has not.

Let me give an example. Suppose you had a bad attack of gallstones and a friend of yours came by to see you at home. You are suffering with unbelievable pain. "Oh, I am sorry you are hurting so much," your friend says. "Do you know Dr. Smith, who is a renowned surgeon for removing the gallbladder?" "Yes, I know him," you reply. "Do you believe that he can perform surgery and get rid of your problem by removing your gallbladder?" "Yes, I do," you reply. "Do you think then you would no longer have pain?" "Yes," you answer. "Then you are cured," he says. "What?" you ask. "You said you believed in him, so you are cured," your friend urges. "What nonsense", you would say. You know you would have to go to the hospital and have surgery before your gallbladder would be removed and you would be free of pain.

What does it mean to believe in Jesus Christ? Does it mean simply to parrot his name? If you say, "Oh, yes, I believe in Jesus," does that insure salvation? Nothing may have really happened in the life of that person. Where there is real healing in a person's life, Jesus Christ reaches into that person's life, and that individual is transformed by Christ, and then he or she commits his or her life to walk daily with Christ. But we have too many who simply have parroted, "Oh, yes I believe," and there is nothing in their lives that indicates that anything real has EVER happened.

A CENTER FOR EXPERIMENTATION

Then the church, if it is to reach young people, will be a *center for experimentation*. It will be an experiential lab where no one will assume that he or she knows the only way to reach people for Christ or how to teach them. The church will try new methods and new ways to open the eyes of people who come to Christ, so they can grow in grace and understanding of the Christian way.

After the French Revolution was over, a man asked an acquaintance, "What did you do during the revolution?" "I survived!" he responded. That may have been quite an accomplishment then. There are times, in certain situations, that to survive is significant. But surely, in the name of God, the church has to do more than survive. It must be an organism that can minister to people. One of the lessons our young adults are trying to teach us today is that they will not trust an institution that does not really care about them. We have to care.

The Problem of Hypocrisy

Secondly, when young adults say they do not trust anybody over thirty, I think they are pointing to the hypocrisy of so much of what we say and do as adults. They declare that you say one thing, but you do another. They say you talk an awful lot about love, but all I see is hate. You say in the church that you are supposed to love one another, but I see more fighting, bigotry, and hatred within the church sometimes than I see in the world. You say that we ought to be united, but I see only divisiveness. You say you are against immorality, but I see you cheating on your wife or your husband. You say we ought to be honest, but I see my parents lying and cheating on their income taxes and manipulating other financial figures to get by dishonestly in life. I hear you saying that you are for peace, but you spend most of your life equipping yourself for war. You say that spiritual values are the most important thing in life, but what I see you giving of all your time and attention to are material ends. Young adults say we are hypocrites.

Now before you write them off and say that is just young people talking, think for a minute. A friend of mine, who is a teacher, said one day a student raised his hand in class and said, "Dr. Brown,

I want to ask a question." The teacher said when that young man asked his question he could feel the hair stand up on the back of his neck. He wanted to say to that student, "You stupid idiot. That is the dumbest question I have ever heard in my life. How can you be in college and ask such a dumb question?" He said it took all the strength within himself not to respond that way. He knew the question was being raised in all seriousness. He knew he had to listen.

Learn to Listen

The church must learn to listen. The church has to listen to young adults and listen to others to hear what their questions are, and then try to respond to the legitimate questions which they raise. Often, we do not. But listen we must! Let's be honest and confess that there are hypocrites in the church. However, we will not let the hypocrites keep us from doing what we know the church should do.

There are also so many concepts of what the church should be like today. Who can determine what is the authentic image of the church? Who in the world has the right one? When people try to speak about the church, it is often like the blind men trying to describe an elephant. One feels only the trunk, another a leg, another the tail, and still another the body. Which blind man has the correct view? Who has the only image of what constitutes the church? We have to search the Scriptures to find the authentic images.

The Importance of a Sense of Humor

I am also convinced that there is no way in the world that anybody can ever survive in ministry in the church today without some sense of humor. There are so many strange things said and done and various interpretations given, that the only response can be laughter. I am convinced that God must have a tremendous sense of humor or else I don't know why God doesn't open a big hole and swallow all of us. God has, I believe, a sense of humor and unconditional love which many of us do not have.

Ministers often hear many unusual things people say to us about our preaching. I have always enjoyed the comment a woman made to her pastor as she came through the door one Sunday. "Oh, Pastor, every sermon you preach is better than the next," she observed. You have to have a sense of humor to stay in ministry, because you never know what people will say or do.

But listen to this: Those who judge the church so harshly for its hypocrites need to be aware that most of the people I know in church are at least trying to live like Christians. They are at least trying! They know they do not always live up to the standards to which they are aspiring, but they are reaching for them. It is so easy to point fingers and condemn people and say, "You are not what a Christian should be!" We know we are not. We have not reached our goal.

Several years ago, at a youth convention, numerous speakers, including a missionary from Africa, had addressed the young people. After the missionary finished speaking, he was having dialogue with the young people. A young man stood up and said, "Listen, all that has gone on here is talk, talk, and more talk. What I want to know is what are you going to do about all these problems?" There was a deathly silence for a while. Finally, the missionary from Africa stood up and said, "I'll tell you what I am going to do. I am going to go back to Africa and continue to serve my God there and minister to the needs of those people." Then he pointed his finger back at that young man and asked: "What are you going to do?"

It is easy, isn't it, to criticize those who are trying to do something for Christ and then just stand back and point fingers, but never get involved?

Is God Over Thirty?

Now look at the question in the subtitle of this chapter. "Is God over thirty?" The scripture passages from Psalm 103: 1-5 give us some insight here. The psalmist declares that God is from everlasting to everlasting. God is the eternal God. Jesus Christ is the

The Rebirth of the Church

same yesterday, today and forever (Hebrews 13:8). We worship an everlasting God, one who is ageless, eternally young. Isaiah writes, "The Lord, the everlasting God, grows neither weary nor faint. He gives vigor to the weary, new strength to the exhausted" (Is. 40: 29-30). This is an everlasting God. Those who commit their lives to God will gain new strength and not be weary or faint.

Both Isaiah and the psalmist use an image familiar to the Jewish people in the image of an eagle. Ancient fables taught that the eagle had a continuous renewal of youth. As one commits his or her life to this God, he or she can fly, run, walk, or even crawl with renewed strength that comes from the everlasting God.

These writers are telling us, I believe, that we can trust God, because God is eternally young. God is eternal — without age, alive in the past and on into the future. God is not over thirty. God is without age — ageless. The eternal God, who is forever young, is calling us to serve him wherever we are and whoever we are-- young, middle aged or old. God is calling us to commit our lives to him and link them in service for him. No matter what our age is we can be young like the God we worship and serve. Not being able to do everything should not keep us from doing something.

When Carlyle Marney was in Lima, Peru one time, he said a Dominican Father came up and spoke with him. "Those of us who think most deeply here in Peru believe that God has given peculiar blessings to your nation; we think she is a land of destiny and high calling. We only wish that her exports matched her calling." Dr. Marney said he reflected on that for some time. Later as he walked around in the marketplace, he saw what the Dominican Father was alluding to. He saw nothing in the market but trinkets, cheap jewelry, and pornographic magazines representing the United States in that country.

Too often what people see representing the Christian faith is only the cheap imitations — pseudo religion, fussing and fighting, and divisiveness. Instead of persons serving God in love, lifting up Christ, giving ourselves in the best way we can with all our strength, we give only trinkets, superficial characteristics, or distorted or valueless images of our faith. We must depict the highest and best of our religion, not the debased or shallow side.

Is God over thirty? Oh, no! God is eternally young. God is also eternally wise, because God is without age. You and I can trust God. We have seen God revealed uniquely in Jesus Christ, who is the same yesterday, today and forever. Remain young by trusting the eternally young God.

11

THE GOSPEL'S CHALLENGE TO YOUNG PEOPLE: AN OPEN LETTER TO BILL AS HE LEAVES FOR COLLEGE

Dear Bill,

It is hard to believe that it is time for you to be leaving home and going to college. Why, it seems like only yesterday that your mother and I went to Rockingham Memorial Hospital in Harrisonburg, Virginia for your birth. I remember waiting in the hallway of the hospital as the doors from the delivery room opened and your mother was wheeled out. Dr. Sease looked at your mother and said, "Now tell him what you have had." She pointed to the doctor and said, "He says it's a boy!" And a boy it was! We brought you home, and you joined your sister on the hillside in Virginia. I remember how easy you were to feed. You always were a good eater, and still are. I remember how well you slept at night and how some of our friends who had a difficult time getting their children to sleep at night were envious that all we had to do was pat you on the back a few moments at night and you would fall asleep and sleep all night. We very seldom had any trouble at night.

As you got to be a toddler, you learned quickly who could be awakened easier in the night. You would slip into our bedroom and tap me on the shoulder, indicate that you had a problem which needed attending to, and daddy would be the one who had to get up in the middle of the night. I remember dressing you in small snow suits, bathing you, and reading stories to you. When you went away from home on a trip with your mother, you began to cry on one occasion, because you were afraid that I was going to finish reading a story to Catherine and you would miss it. I had to promise you that I would wait until you came home before I read any more of *The Wizard of Oz*.

One day, when you were small, your mother told me that she couldn't find you. She looked frantically for you through the neighborhood. She called and called you without response. Finally, she saw you pushing yourself along in your little toy car on the lower side of the circle. As she came running up to you, you said: "Mother, I been looking for you." But not as hard as she had been looking for you!

I remember the toy lawn mower that you used to push as you walked beside me as I cut the grass. I remember when we moved to Bristol and the heavy snow that fell on our first Christmas there. We all went out and played in the snow. Instead of making a snowman, we sculptured a huge snow duck. We were the envy of the neighborhood with our masterpiece, and you were so proud of your creation on that Christmas day. I remember the hikes that you and I used to take up into the hills behind our house. I remember the haircut your sister gave you. It wasn't exactly a professional job, and your mother and I wondered if it would ever grow back. I remember the time you fell and bumped your head on our brick wall and got two black eyes. The folks at church wondered what we were doing to you.

I will never forget the time when you got in the car parked in the driveway on the hillside with your sister and tried to drive it. You slipped the car out of park and went down the hill backwards. Fortunately, you turned the wheel and it went across the front lawn and then rolled back into a small dogwood tree which I had planted the night before. That small tree stopped the car from rolling down the hill and crashing into the house across the street. I was happy to give up that dogwood tree to have both of you.

I recall putting together toys for you at Christmas time and sometimes wondered if I would ever get some of them put together.

I remember trying to teach you how to ride a bicycle. You would have it balanced perfectly, but, as soon as I would let go of the bicycle, you would throw your feet off the pedals, and I would have to grab the bike again. I will never forget the tree house that you and I worked so hard to build. You loved to play and sleep in it. I remember the tool box you made and how you used it as a school project. I remember our attempts at trying to catch fish in those mountain streams in Virginia and Tennessee and how difficult it always seemed to be to catch anything. Our luck never seemed to be too good. I will never forget the times we would go swimming and you and your sister would yell: "Throw me!" I laugh as I think about the time you were the "third" skunk in "100 Per Cent Chance of Rain."

I remember when you went into the lawn mowing business one summer. You made enough money to buy your first skis and put enough money in the bank to go skiing in the winter. I remember your baseball and basketball games. I remember your job at Bonn Pharmacy and your difficult construction job. I remember your first date. I remember teaching you how to drive the car. In my scrapbook of memories, I shall always be able to see you coming down the church aisle with your sister on your arm for her wedding.

Oh, there are so many memories I could pick out of the scrapbook of memories. In a brief letter like this it is hard for me to know where to focus. It's a time of letting go. It is never easy for parents to let go, because we want our umbilical cord to hang on for a long time. The desire is often to hold on too long, to want to continue to guide you, and to help too much.

There will be some things I'm not so sure we really will miss. It will seem strange not to have your big tennis shoes in the den to trip over, or the sound of your loud music. In fact, a caller might be able to get a telephone call through. And when the phone rings now, it will be for your mother or me. But most of all you will leave a void, and we will miss you. There are a few things I would really like to write to you in this letter, but I don't have time to address them all. It would take a long time to say all I would really like to say. There are, however, a few things I do want you to remember as you leave home and go to college.

This is a time of new beginning for you. It will be a new chapter in your life. A new world lies before you. I know it will be an exciting time for you. I hope it will be a good adventure. In some ways there are many things that are frightening about leaving home. Once you go off to college and come back home again, it is never quite the same. We know that, you will discover that soon. You are beginning to let go and so are we. Our nest will soon be empty.

Although the future is unknown, I hope you will face this new adventure with anticipation. You have the opportunity to make of your life whatever you want. I wish I could tell you everything that is going to happen to you in the future or tell you where you could find out what is going to happen to you, but I can't. There is no crystal ball, fortune teller, Ouija board, or horoscope that can give you a guarantee about tomorrow. You go into the future searching, groping, and praying. I wish I could tell you how you can know exactly what God wants you to do with your life, or how you can always understand what his guidance is. The writer in Proverbs has stated: "In all your ways acknowledge him and he will direct your path" (Proverbs 3: 6). I hope you will do that. But honestly it is not always easy to know what God's direction is. There have been times I have struggled to know God's guidance and I wanted to say: "God turn on a bright light. Give me a telephone call. Give me signal." But it has not always been that clear for me.

One of the things I have discovered is that God will not violate my own freedom. He has not made you or me like a robot. God will not manipulate you. He gives you the right to say yes or no, to choose a lower path or a higher way. He will give you the freedom to make decisions — right ones or bad ones. I hope that you will let him cast his light on your pathway. Whenever I have searched for God's guidance, I have always heard him respond to me by saying: "Walk in the light you already have. Follow the knowledge that you understand in this moment. Walk in that light."

Do you remember the small miner's lantern we have on the bookshelf in the den that used to belong to your grandfather? Maybe that could be a parable for us. A miner would attach that lantern to his hard hat and go deep into the coal mine. He would turn the light on and shine the beam of light a short distance in front of him and then walk in that light. As he walked in the light right before him, he was able to go further.

As you move into the future, walk in the light that you see in front of you. You will never be able to see all the way to the end of your path. Walk in whatever light you have. As you follow in that light, God will give you more light, and insight along the path. I hope you will seek to follow the light that God will give you.

Knowledge can become a key to unlock many doors for you. You go to school to prepare yourself to be better educated. The word "educate" comes from a Latin word which means "to make a plant grow." Growth is a sign of life. Green leaves indicate life on a tree. If you are not growing, you are not alive. A truly educated person does not know what it is to be bored. He or she is always open and growing. I hope you will discover in a new way the significance of reading. Reading can open whole new worlds which lie before you. Remember that you will never arrive educationally. You are always in process of learning. I hope that you will increase in your wisdom and knowledge as Jesus did.

Do not be afraid of facing tough questions that might challenge your faith. Do not let science, philosophy, or anything make you fearful for your faith. Your faith can stand any kind of tough questions, and you need not be afraid of them. Always have a tough mind but a tender heart. Don't avoid wrestling with difficult questions, because your faith will grow in your struggle with them. We trust a God who will sustain us in all circumstances.

As you seek to acquire knowledge, remember that knowledge is not just having a lot of facts. Information is not enough. There are some students who can memorize geometry or math theories, but they really don't have any idea how the principles behind these theories work. Try to learn the "why" and "how" of things. A real knowledge of history is not merely the memorization of a lot of facts. Try to learn the causes behind significant historical movement. When you learn the principles and causes behind your facts, your information will be more meaningful. Some facts are essential for education, but don't be satisfied with facts alone.

You may have read about the man who was called in by a large electrical company because they could not find anyone to repair the huge machine that operated the plant. The company had brought in "experts" and spent a small fortune trying to repair the machine, but to no avail. Finally, they called in a man who was considered <u>the</u> expert in such matters. He came to the plant and listened to the machine for a while, examined a few parts, and then told the officials to turn it on again. He then took out his hammer and tapped on it in two places, and the machine began to hum perfectly. He sent them a bill of $5000 for his few minutes of work. The manager demanded that the expert itemize his bill. He did. He sent a bill which read: "For tapping on the machine twice — $1.00. For knowing where to tap- $4999.00."

Try to get inside your information so it can be useful to you in life. You will need to know some facts, but you will discover that real knowledge is more than the acquiring of a list of the right facts. The important thing is not always how much you know but how you use what you know.

Be willing to learn from other people. Don't assume that you already know everything. Too many people, especially students, approach life with this attitude. They assume that they already know what they need to learn and are not willing to be open to new truths. Ask questions if you don't understand something. Push your professor so that he or she will share his understanding of the truth or give you a clearer perspective into seeing it. Ask questions. It is the path to knowledge. Be willing to grow in your knowledge.

I told you how I learned to ride a bicycle when I was a small boy. I had watched other boys and girls ride their bicycles for some time. I decided that I could do that, too. One day I picked up a bicycle of a friend of mine and started pedaling. Sure enough I found I could balance it perfectly, and down the street I went. I was so proud of myself, and I was doing a great job until I started down a hill. Children began to yell, "Put on the brakes! Put on the brakes!" Adults began to run beside me shouting: "Put on the brakes." But I didn't know how to put on the brakes! I finally came to a stop when I ran head-on into a parked car. I was thrown up on top of the car and luckily received only a bloody nose.

My problem was that I thought I already knew how to ride a bicycle. I had not been willing to let somebody else teach me how to use the brakes and learn the other information that would have made my riding of the bicycle easier. I hope you will be willing to learn from others. It is better to acquire some of our knowledge from others than to have to learn it from bad experience.

Gerald Kennedy had an uncle whom many considered a wise man. Somebody asked him one day how he got to be so wise. "I've got good judgment," he replied. "Good judgment comes from experience. And experience — well — that comes from poor judgment."

Unfortunately, the only way some people ever seem to learn is from poor judgment. Why don't you learn some things from other people who have already experienced difficulties and accomplishments? Let them teach you. You don't have to learn everything firsthand. I encourage you to be willing to be open and learn that way.

I also hope that you will not be discouraged easily. Life is crowded with cynics and pessimists. Many persons are filled with gloom, despair, and cynicism. These negative persons can always tell you what is wrong with everything in life, and why something won't work. They often live out their lives in despair, hopelessness, and usually end up quitting whatever they start. You will have some of your school friends who will tell you that your teacher is not any good, and that you can't learn anything from him. Every teacher you have will not be the best in the world. They may not all be A-plus. But I have discovered that you can learn from every kind of teacher, if you are willing to put forth your best effort. Don't let fellow students or poor teachers discourage you.

George Bernard Shaw once wrote, "Do you know what a pessimist is? A pessimist is a man who thinks everybody is as nasty as himself and hates them for it." Don't go through life with that kind of attitude. Learn to be positive. Our day is a time for optimism, enthusiasm, and affirmation. Approach your life with hope and excitement.

Don't be discouraged when sometimes you don't succeed, because no person succeeds at everything he or she does. Everybody fails at something sometime or another. But learn from your failures and build on them to be a better person. Columbus struggled for years to get somebody to finance his trip to the new world. But nobody was interested. One day, when he and his young son stopped to get some water at a monastery, he poured out his problem to a monk. The monk later talked to the queen, and she gave Columbus an audience. He had failed in his earlier tries to get her ear. Edison failed in far more of his efforts than he succeeded when he labored to discover new inventions. Learn that mistakes and failures are not the end. Failing is not a sin, but it is a sin not to be willing to try at all. Failure may close one door, but what you learn may open another door.

Several years ago, a professor at MIT, who taught a course on "Failure," was interviewed on *The Today Show*. He noted that too much emphasis was placed on success in our country. He felt that people needed to be taught how to deal with failure, since we usually fail in more ways than we succeed. At the conclusion of the interview, the professor was asked: "Well, did anybody fail your course?" "No," he said, "but I had two incompletes." There are a lot of incompletes and failures in life. But learn from those, and build on them, and go on. Don't let the things you were not able to accomplish discourage you or crush your hopes and dreams. Press forward.

I want to encourage you not to let other people determine your behavior. Oh, it is easy isn't it, to let the crowd influence exactly how you live and act in everything you attempt to do. Learn the art of self-control. Learn to control situations and not be controlled by them.

A newspaper boy once insulted a Quaker. He responded graciously to the paper carrier. "I don't understand," somebody said to him, "why you acted like you did toward this young boy, when he was so ugly to you." "I have learned," the Quaker replied, "never to let somebody else's behavior determine my own."

What an insight into life that is. It is not easy to do. When somebody treats you in an ugly way, treat them kindly. Never let somebody else's bad behavior determine who you are and how you will respond.

In my grandmother's Bible, as I have told you before, there is a line which she wrote many years ago: "He who would teach others, must first master himself." I hope you will learn self-discipline. Learn to discipline yourself in such a way that you will be able to respond to others out of the finest qualities that you possess. Self-discipline will help you to be the kind of student and person you need to be in life. I trust you will learn to discover who you really are. There are a lot of people who go through life asking: "Who is this I, me, you, they, he, she? Who am I really?"

Have you ever read about the processionary caterpillar? This caterpillar links itself to the caterpillar right in front of it, and the next one links itself to the one in front of it, and so on. If you place these caterpillars on the top of a pan or a tin can, they will continue to go around in a circle, one linked to the other, until they drop from exhaustion and die.

Too often we live that way, don't we? We simply follow what everybody else is doing. You will find strong peer pressure to violate your high, moral values. I hope you will not merely follow the leader. Worldly Wisdom will push its head up and say: "I can give you the insights to teach you how to be a clever person who can manipulate, use, and abuse others and make you rich." Macho Materialism will lift its strong hand to try to tell you that the only thing worthwhile in life is to get possessions and to have money.

Pleasant Pleasures will tell you, as it caresses your brow, that sex, drugs, and alcohol are the only worthwhile things in life, so get your fill of them now. I hope you will not be like the caterpillars and simply follow the easy path of conformity.

Remember who you are. Do you remember the phrase we used to use when you would leave the house with your friends or go on a date: "Remember who you are!" You are a child of God. You are our son. You are a Christian. You have been created with high values, given high standards and high principles. When the world seeks to drag you down to its paths, remember who you are. Hopefully, that memory will be able to carry you through the difficult, rough spots of life. I hope it will remind you of your deeper source of strength. You have values and principles deep within that can help carry you through your trials.

I hope that you will reach for the highest you can be. Cling to a high vision of life. Try to be the very best person you can in whatever vocation you choose. Reach for the highest standards that you can possibly attain. Strive to be the best that you can be in whatever goal you aim for. Ask yourself a question: "What do I want to be more than anything else?"

Frederic W. Boatwright, who was president of the University of Richmond, my alma mater, for fifty-one years, fell into a millstream when he was a young child and was swept through a culvert. They later pulled him out of the water and pronounced him dead. They placed him on a bed, but that night he suddenly awakened. Later he went on to accomplish some significant things in the realm of education. Somebody once asked him about his philosophy of life. "Give yourself," he said, "to something that will outlast you."

I hope you will do that. Material things will not accomplish that goal. I want you to make a good income, because I don't want to support you all your life. But I hope that material ends will not be your only goal in life.

Remember how you and Catherine used to joke about my "Ticket Please" sermon that you heard so much. I hope you will remember some things from that "Ticket Please" sermon. One of the things I hope you will always remember which I stressed in that sermon is that you do not find life meaningful, but you make it meaningful. I want you to remember that Jesus Christ has called you not merely to try to get something for yourself but to spend your life, to invest it, and give your life in service and ministry for others. Whatever vocation you may choose, I hope a part of your job will be to try and help meet the needs of people. Listen to the cries of hurting humanity and respond in some way to help answer that call.

In your reach for a high vision, I encourage you to let worship have a significant place. I know that college is sometimes a difficult place for a student to keep up his worship habits as he should. But I hope you will always remember that the roots of religion are deep within your life. Remember Christ who will lead you and care for you. Don't forget that prayer will undergird you in times when you are alone. Continue to nourish your spiritual life. Don't be ashamed of your spiritual heritage. Throughout your years in college, nurture and fortify your spiritual life. Let Jesus Christ be your model. Strengthen your relationship with Jesus Christ as Lord, and like him, may you increase in wisdom, in stature, and in favor with God and man.

Leonard Griffith told about a visit he made once to a museum in London. Some blind students came into the museum to "look" at the Greek statues. He said he noticed a tall, skinny blind boy as he felt the huge, massive muscles of the athletic figure of the discus thrower. He saw the boy's back straighten up and saw his shoulders go back as he sought to measure up to that model.

Like the blind boy, we all measure ourselves by many models. Let the paramount model in your life be Jesus Christ, our Lord and Savior. Seek to live up to his ideals, principles, and goals. Strive to follow him in all that you do.

Now in closing I want you to remember that your mother and I will always be here, if you need us. All you have to do is write or call. We want to give a willing ear. We will always be open to whatever need you have. You are moving toward independence, and we want to help in any and every way we can. Remember that we love you more than you can ever realize. Your mother and I care for you deeply. We hope that your life will be filled with much happiness and meaning. May God bless you.

    Love,
    Dad

12

Going Home Again

A noted fiction critic has observed, "Most novels are about going home or leaving home." I believe I understand something of this critic's thrust. Emily and I moved to Richmond about eighteen years ago to be near our daughter, Catherine Whitty, her husband, John, and our three grandchildren, J. T., Emily, and Michael. We had to start "going home" in a completely new place. In our married life, Emily and I have probably moved about ten times. If you have moved a lot, you understand the frustrations moving can engender. Someone has observed that "Hell is not a place but a moving van."

Several years ago, I had to go back to my hometown and to the house where I grew up to undertake the final task of determining what to do with my parents' possessions and how to divide them with my brother and sister. My mother died at 85 years old in 1996. She was my last surviving parent. My father had died three years earlier at the age of 85. Selling my parents' house and leaving was not easy. This had been my home place since I was a small boy. When I went back for Christmas or for other visits, I slept in the same bed which had been mine for over half a century. Now, this chapter in my life has come to a close. The house has been sold and has gone into the hands of somebody else. I will indeed not be able to go home again.

Oh, I know, over fifty years ago I established my own home when I married Emily. I moved out of that Lynchburg, Virginia, house, and it became a place which I visited. But can I so quickly cut off the memories, the impact that this home had upon my life? Can I forget the home where, as a boy, I rode stick horses like great stallions as I played cowboys and Indians with my brother and other friends in our neighborhood? Can I forget the small forts we built piled high with rocks and leaves placed inside for a carpet? Or the battles we fought with raging Indians? I am a part of that home in so many ways: the neighbors whose grass I cut, the gardens we tended by our house, the lake which I walked around, fished in, and swam in as a boy; the pickup baseball, basketball, and football games we played on our little piece of turf; and the horseshoe pitching contest in which I became proficient. I am still a part of those long walks to school and church, bike rides to the store, and meals around the family table.

This Lynchburg home will always be to me a place where I learned high moral principles, the value of hard work, the importance of discipline, integrity, religion, love, good manners and how to get along with my fellow human beings. Nor will I ever forget how exciting my mother made Christmas. It was a grand event. Our home was always decorated with colored lights, a cedar tree, greenery and the smell of cakes, pies and food of all kinds tantalized the senses. I guess I will always see my mother as a beautiful woman in her forties standing stately and well dressed. I see my father with his mail carrier's bag on his back, his hat pulled down on his flattop silver hair. I can't go home again and be a boy and share in the mischievous pranks at Halloween and other times with my brother, nor tease my sister, nor sit on my grandfather's lap.

My brother, Preston, who was a painting contractor painted my parent's house and then we sold it easily. I went back to Lynchburg and made a final visit to the house that had been my home and my parents' home for at least 55 years. I walked through the empty house. This was the first time I had ever seen the house without furniture. After my brief tour through the house, I sat down on the steps and offered a prayer of thanksgiving for the role this house, my parents and family, had played in my life. I thanked God for my parents, who had both lived to be 85, and for the love, guidance and support they had given me. I prayed for guidance as I sought to live the rest of my life as husband, father, and grandfather.

I know that I have come to a point in my life that I have closed the door to a chapter in my home life which can never be opened again in the same way. For me there is a sense of genuine sadness in that. But there is also a quest to know how to draw upon the resources that I had in that home and how I might be a better person myself because of them.

THE SEARCH FOR HOME

I believe that much of life is spent in searching for a home — a place where we feel secure, accepted, and loved. There is that deep longing in all of us for home. Yet, in a sense, all of us have a sense of homelessness. Even if we have a place called home, for many of us there is still a searching, yearning, groping, pulling toward something beyond, something not located in a place. I think that life is a journey in search of a home. It is a pilgrimage to go home again. The search for home, I believe, is a religious quest.

WHERE IS HOME?

IS IT IN THE PAST?

Where do we find "home?" Is home found in the past? Now that I have closed my parents' home, there is that pull toward the past. When I talk with some of our elderly members, especially those in nursing homes or those whose spouse is deceased, there is a longing to go back to the past. Life for many is only seen in the past and not in the present.

As we went through my parents' possessions, like all children we had to make decisions about what we would keep, give away or sell. These were not easy decisions. One night we were going through the attic and we discovered many boxes of cards that my mother had kept through the years. On some of them she had written, "I could not throw these away." Our first inclination was simply to pitch all these boxes. But Emily encouraged us not to and so later that night we sat down in the floor and went through those boxes. We discovered cards and notes that our children had written to their grandparents when our children were very small. We discovered poems that my brother had written to our parents when he was young and even when he was older. We divided many of these cards and notes into special piles for each family and collected them. We noted the sentimental valentines and love notes that my parents had sent to each other. It carried us back to our own past as well as the past of my parents.

I discovered in one box a little soldier's uniform and a pilgrim outfit that my mother had made for me when I was in kindergarten or the first or second grade. Every box, drawer or closet we opened or looked in took us on a nostalgic trip. These were possessions that had been a part of my parents' life and some of them in my own life. This was a trip back to familiar and nostalgic times which cannot be recaptured again.

As important as my home was to me in the past and yours to you, we cannot go back to that home today. We can build on the foundation that we received there. But I do not believe that home is found in the past.

Is Our Home in the Future?

For some home is seen primarily in the future. It is a dream, a longing, a myth, and a desire to have some place where one is not homeless but has arrived. It is something for which a person lives in anticipation, but realization has not come about yet. The Heaven's Gate cult a decade or so ago was looking for such a future home. They felt it was to be found on some spaceship behind the comet, Hale-Bopp. This cult was so sure of its existence that they willingly took their own lives — laid down the "vessels," they said, that contained their souls, so they might go on to that home in the future.

I believe without question there is a future dimension to the quest for home. But most of us are not homesick yet. There is

The Rebirth of the Church

something unnatural, almost unreal, if one's focus is only toward the future and he or she dismisses the present.

LIFE IS A JOURNEY SEARCHING FOR HOME

I believe that life is made up of moving toward home or seeking to go home again. Life is a journey seeking to find our way home. This is seldom an easy quest. "Home is both the beginning and the end. Home is not a sentimental journey at all," Richard Rohr declares, "but an inner compass and a North Star at the same time. It is a metaphor for the soul."[17]

Frederick Buechner, in one of his novels entitled "Treasure Hunt" (in *The Book of Bebb)*, speaks through a young man named Antonio Parr, the narrator, who has been away from home for several weeks. When he returns home, he finds that his son and some other children have made a sign which reads "WELCOME HONE." The last leg of the *"m"* in home is missing so that it turns into "hone." "It seems oddly fitting," Antonio Parr says when he first sees the sign. "It was good to get home, but it was home with something missing or out of whack about it. It wasn't much, to be sure, just a minor stoke or serif, but even a minor stoke can make a major difference."

A little later he remembers a second time the sign which met him when he arrived home. He continues, "WELCOME HONE" the sign said, and I can't help thinking again of Gideon and Barak, of Samson and David and all the rest of the crowd . . . who, because some small but crucial thing was missing, kept looking for it, come hell or high water. Wherever they went till their eyes were dim and their arches fallen."[18]

Buechner says the reference here is to the 11th chapter of the Letter to the Hebrews where the writer lists the great heroes and heroines of biblical faith but then adds, "These all died in faith, not

---

17 Richard Rohr, *Falling Upward: A Spirituality for the Two Halves of Life* (San Francisco: Jossey-Bass, 2011), xxxvii.
18 Frederick Buechner, *The Book of Bebb* (San Francisco: Harper Collins,1999), 529.

having received what was promised, but having seen it and greeted it from afar, and having acknowledged that they were strangers and exiles on the earth. For people who speak thus make it clear that they are seeking a homeland" (Hebrews 11:13-14).[19]

WE ARE PILGRIMS — SOJOURNERS

The picture in the book of Hebrews depicts a pilgrim, a sojourner or a foreigner who is on a continuous pilgrimage searching for a permanent home. He or she seemed to be a resident alien, one who was an outsider — a stranger without permanent lodging, without a home, traveling in a strange land, looking for that home which somehow lay before him or her. These patriarchs of the faith, however, lived not in despair but in hope. They knew rejection, abuse, persecution, suffering and ridicule. But they continued to follow the God who went before them.

Jill McCorkle grew up in Lumberton, North Carolina, and First Baptist Church, where I served as Pastor. She has now become a noted Southern writer. Several ago she received the Hobson Prize at Chowan College. In her reception speech she spoke about Tom Lowe, one of the characters in her novel, *Carolina Moon*. He was the owner of a piece of beachfront property which now, because of Hurricane Hazel, was under water except at low tide. She indicated that she put that character in her book because he was a reminder of the uncertainty of life. Tom's father had purchased a piece of property on which he was going to build a beachfront house. But before he could, Hazel changed the oceanfront and he discovered that his property was under water part of the time. He continued to pay his $72.00 a year tax. Tom came down almost every day and spent a short period of time standing on his piece of property when it was low tide.[20]

---

19 Frederick Buechner, *The Longing for Home* (San Francisco: Harper Collins, 1996), 17- 18.
20 Helmut Thielicke, *Being a Christian When the Chips Are Down* (Philadelphia: Fortress Press, 1979), 45.

LIFE IS UNCERTAIN

The journey through life is indeed uncertain. It is filled with ups and downs, happiness and sadness, good times and bad times, celebrations and heartaches, failures, and festivities. The Christian has no promise that along this journey he or she may not have difficulties and experience the unexpected. What we do have is the promise that we do not travel alone. There is nothing that separates us from God when we are in Christ Jesus our Lord. (Romans 8:35-39)

TRAVEL HOPEFULLY

Despite all the difficulties that the patriarchs experienced, they never turned back. They marched from the deserts of Egypt toward the Promised Land. They traveled with a vision before their eyes and hope in their hearts. Although the journey had been difficult, they did not cease traveling toward their destination. "It is better to travel hopefully than to arrive," Robert Lewis Stevenson once wrote. They never reached the end of their journey, but they traveled with hope and expectation, not growing weary in their travels, but fortified by the assurance of God.

GOING HOME AGAIN

Thomas Wolfe wrote, "You Can't Go Home Again." I wonder if that is true. I want to encourage us to think about some ways that we can go home again. At Christmastime the question heard on many lips is, "Are you going home for Christmas?" I know that question usually refers to a place, but I think that I would encourage you to go home again in a different sense. I hope that you will return to an earlier stage in your life — not physically go home. But return to some place or some time in your life where you can recapture the rich meaning from your past. Go home again and recapture your lost ideals and lost dreams. Look once again for the star that captured you with its glow when you were young and follow it to a new horizon. Go back to some of your youthful aspirations, youthful goals, to those times in your life when you dreamed dreams. Go home again and seek to find those things which enriched your life. If you are young, hang on to your dreams.

Recapture Your Dreams

Many of us have turned away from the dreams, ideals, goals, and callings which we felt as young men and women. Somehow, someway, we need to travel home again and recover those important values that may have become lost.

Charles Rice said that one day he was riding the subway toward mid-Manhattan and looked up at the marquee and saw the first sign of the Christmas season. The poster had depicted an old wooden child's sleigh, trimmed in red, and surrounded by snow. Underneath the picture were two lines which read, "Remember when this was the only thing you wanted in the whole world?"[21]

I am not encouraging you or myself just to take a nostalgic trip. But some of us need to reach back and remember some of those earlier dreams, ideals, goals and hopes that we may have lost. Some of these are dreams or ideals we had for our family, our marriage, our work, and our own ethical value. Maybe it is time we went home again and recaptured those ideals. Helmut Thielicke, the German theologian, wrote, "Blessed are they who have a native land, for they may go home again."[22] We can go home to God and recapture those things that have been lost. Christ gives us an opportunity to begin again.

A Place to Belong

Take another step with me and see if we cannot go home again to discover that there is a place where we belong. Too many of us live rootless lives. Going home again is reaching back to our

---

21 Charles Rice, "Watch Therefore," The Twentieth Century Pulpit, vol. II, edited by James W. Cox (Nashville: Abingdon Press, 1981), 158.
22 Paul Tillich, *The Shaking of the Foundations* (New York: Charles Scribner's Sons, 1948), 162.

roots and tying ourselves to family and friends so we can find our identity again. People feel deep pain and hurt when they feel they no longer have family. When death, distance or divorce separates them from family, they often feel homeless, rejected, or isolated. Probably one of the worse struggles that any person goes through is that feeling of not being loved or accepted.

As we looked through picture albums in my parents' home, I felt a strong tug back to the past. I sensed once again the significance of family roots and continuity. But on a deeper level we all need to be reminded that we are tied in with the family of God. We belong. We are not isolated, fragmented egos, but we belong to the family of God. That gives us a rich continuity. We are a part of the pilgrims of faith through the centuries. Paul Tillich has reminded us to "accept our acceptance by God."[6] God loves us. As the prodigal son was welcomed home from his far country, so God welcomes and accepts us all home again.

A Longing for Relationship

Take with me now another important step in this journey of faith toward home. Maybe being a part of the family of God is not so much a place of lodging as it is a relationship. We travel towards home to find acceptance, security, love, a sense of family and the freedom to be ourselves. This may be best realized, not so much in a place, as in a quality of life. It is relational, not merely a place to hang your hat. Going home again is a quest for belonging, identification. It is a state of being connected, connected to God. A state of becoming — becoming a more mature Christian — a more authentic human being.

We love to sing Martin Luther's great hymn, "A Mighty Fortress Is Our God, a Bulwark Never Failing." But is this magnificent hymn about our faith primarily about a place or about a relationship or a state of being? Does not the promise from Jesus that, "I will never leave you or forsake you," assure us that we are not homeless? The One who is the resurrection and the life is there with us to travel in our pilgrimage through life. There are people who have several homes in this country and in other places in the world, but they are really homeless. They are not at home in any of them. No one is truly at peace until he or she has found peace in God.

A house was hit by a storm one afternoon and all the windows and doors in that house were rattling. A young boy in the house rushed to his father and exclaimed, "Daddy, Daddy, it sounds like someone is knocking at every door we have."

A Beckoning to the "Not Yet Realized"

I believe that in the journey of life God continuously knocks at every door of our life seeking to come in. God wants to bring us out of the damp basement of depression and despair or out of the attic of memories and regrets into the brightness of the life that lies before us. In going home again the direction is never back to the past to remain there. But to learn from the past and move towards the future which is beckoning us eternally onward to the not yet, to the more than, other than we are — to be more like God. Jesus said, "I have gone to prepare a place for you and that where I am there you may be also." The journey toward home will eventually take us toward that heavenly home. But we know that going home again is okay as long as we walk with Christ.

Anne Lamott tells the story about a two-year-old child who accidentally locked himself in a room one night. His mother heard him call out to her, "Mommy! Mommy!" The mother discovered that she could not open the door from the outside and she told her child several times, "Just jiggle the door knob, honey." The child, frightened and crying, did not understand. Unable to open the door herself, the mother didn't know what to do. Finally, she fell on her knees and slid her fingers beneath the door in the space between the bottom of the door and the floor. She instructed her son to kneel until he could feel her fingers. After searching for a while, he felt them, and he stayed like that for some time, simply holding her fingers in the dark. After he stopped crying and had calmed down, the mother gently said to him, "Now stand up and jiggle the door knob." He stood up and did as his mother instructed and the door popped open.[23]

Like the image of the child's fingers under the door grasping his mother's fingers in the darkness, when I am in my low moments of life and God seems hidden behind some door or I have locked myself in a room of confusion, deceit, depression, sinfulness, or misdirection, I grope for the fingers (presence) of God. The presence of God often seems illusive. Even when I cannot sense God's presence, the Scriptures assure me that God is there, nevertheless. God beckons to us to come home again. God reaches motherly/fatherly fingers toward us and invites us back home again, assuring us that God has never left us nor forsaken us.

So, go home again. The door is open, and the light is on.

---

23 Anne Lamott, *Operating Instructions: A Journal of My Son's First Year* (New York, Fawcett Columbine, 1993), 220-21.

13

Like a Mighty Army

Jimmy Mitchell was back home after serving two years in the army. His home pastor asked him if he would speak in the morning service. At first, he refused, but then, with a funny light in his eyes, he said he would if the congregation would sing "Onward, Christian Solders" right before he spoke. His pastor agreed. After the congregation finished singing, Jimmy began by saying: "You have been singing 'Like a mighty army moves the church of God.' That might have been all right once. The trouble is now that just about ten million men know exactly how an army moves. And it doesn't move the way a lot of you folks at St. John's do — or do not. Suppose the army accepted the lame excuses that many of you people think are good enough to serve as an alibi for not attending Church Parade."

"Imagine this, if you can. Reveille seven a.m. Squads on the parade ground. The sergeant barks out, "Count fours." "One!" "Two!" "Three!" Number Four missing. "Where's Private Smith?" "Oh," pipes up a chap by the vacant place. "Mr. Smith was too sleepy to get up this morning. He was out late last night and needed the sleep. He said to tell you that he would be with you in spirit." "That's fine," says the sergeant. "Remember me to him." "Where's Brown?" asks the sergeant. "Oh," puts in another chap, "he's out playing golf. He gets only one day a week for recreation, and you know how important that is." "Sure, sure," is the sergeant's cheerful answer. "Hope he has a good game".

"Where's Robinson?" "Robinson," explains a buddy, "is sorry not to greet you in person. But he is entertaining guests today and of course couldn't come. Besides, he was at drill last week." "Thank you," says the sergeant, smiling. "Tell him he is welcome any time he is able to drop in."

"Honest, now, did any conversation like that ever happen in any army? Don't make me laugh. If any G.I. tried to pull that stuff, he would get twenty days in the guardhouse. Yet you hear stuff like that every week in the church, and said with a straight face, too. "Like a mighty army. Why, if St. John's really moved like a mighty army, a lot of you folks would be court-martialed!"[24]

The church today seldom moves like a mighty army. But well it should. The local church is the headquarters for the army of Christ. It is the base of operations, the drill camp, the hospital for the wounded and the hurting, the center for training and the place for equipping to minister and serve in the world.

Many church members turn to the church only when they want to get married or buried or have a crisis in their lives. These same people often show greater loyalty to their civic clubs or country clubs where they have annual dues and attendance requirements. The church must assume some of the responsibility for this failing since it has placed too much emphasis on the ease of church membership and has not had any real requirements for those who have joined. There has been too much stress on the security of the believer and not enough acknowledgement of faithfulness. Many have found cheap grace from their church and have been unwilling to examine the New Testament requirements for following Christ. This failing demands that we look again at the New Testament call to discipleship.

Dietrich Bonhoeffer has called this "cheap grace." "Cheap grace," according to Bonhoeffer, "is the preaching of forgiveness without requiring repentance, baptism without church discipline, communion without confession, absolution without personal con-

---

[24] Robert E. Luccock (ed), *Halford Luccock Treasury.* (New York: Abingdon Press, 1963), 346-347.

The Rebirth of the Church

fession. Cheap grace is grace without discipleship, grace without the cross, grace without Jesus Christ, living and incarnate."[25]

Those who wanted cheap grace have joined a church before they were ready to commit themselves to Christ. They have looked for comfort, ease, an air-conditioned place to worship, and a religion with few or no demands. Any time things become difficult or problems emerge, they have fled to another church with fewer demands or hardships.

Christ, however, has challenged us to a real commitment. He invites us to join a disciplined army of those who are willing to train and serve in his name. Few really want that kind of demand. He requires of us commitment, discipline, time, loyalty, faithfulness and not a superficial relationship. Listen to Bonhoeffer again. "Costly grace is the treasure hidden in the field; for the sake of it a man will gladly go and sell all that he has. It is the pearl of great price to buy which the merchant will sell all his goods. It is the regal rule of Christ, for whose sake a man will pluck out the eye which causes him to stumble, it is the call of Jesus Christ at which the disciple leaves his nets and follows him." Bonhoeffer goes even further when he declares:

> Costly grace is the gospel which must be sought repeatedly, the gift which must be asked for, the door at which a man must knock.
>
> Such grace is costly because it calls us to follow, and it is grace because it calls us to follow *Jesus Christ*. It is costly because it costs a man his life, and it is grace because it gives a man the only true life. It is *costly* because it condemns sin, and grace because it justifies the sinner. Above all, it is costly because it cost God the life of his Son: 'ye were bought at a price', and what has cost God much cannot be cheap for us. Above all, it is *grace* because God did not reckon his Son too

---

25   Dietrich Bonhoeffer, *The Cost of Discipleship*, (London: SCM Press, 1959), 36.

dear a price to pay for our life but delivered him up for us. Costly grace is the Incarnation of God.[26]

The Apostle Paul had preached about such grace, but he was also willing to pay the price with his own life. In his letter to young Timothy, he urged him to be willing to "share in suffering like a good soldier of Christ Jesus" (2 Timothy 2:3). At the time of the writing of the Letter to the Ephesians, he had been imprisoned in a Roman jail for three years chained to a Roman soldier. He drew his image of the Christian soldier from the Roman soldier he saw day after day. This letter was his Epistle of Captivity.

The Character of the Enemy

Paul begins in Ephesians 6:10-17 by describing the character of the enemy which the Christian is engaging. He acknowledges the continuous presence and power of the forces of evil in the world. He attests that the Christian and the church are always under attack from the forces of evil. The Christian life is a constant warfare against evil. In his day, Paul saw these forces of evil as demonic and spiritual in nature. Today we are likely to sense the demonic power deep within ourselves and in the corrupt forces of society.

We do acknowledge that evil is real! We see the power of evil in the life of a teenager caught under the hypnotic stare of drugs. Its evidence is visible in the college student who is paralyzed for life. Its power is seen in the continuous piling of atomic weapons, the threats of terrorists, the Arab-Israeli struggle, the corruption in business and politics, and in the sexual distortions on TV, in the movies, the internet, and in many magazines.

We can look into the dark abyss of our own souls and we recognize the power of evil. We know our own selfishness, envy, jealousy, vindictiveness, lust, sexual passions, and lying. There is darkness within us as well as around us.

Paul also alerts us to the fact that evil comes upon us unexpectedly and without warning. Evil gives no early warning signals — no

---

26   Ibid., 36-37.

emergency storm signs. We hear its roar and the beast is upon us. Like a match thrown into combustible material, the flame ignites without alerting us first. Temptations come upon us "like a thief in the night." Its presence seduces us when we least expect it. Our struggle with evil is personal and comes to us like two soldiers engaged in hand to hand combat.

A Call to Prepare

Paul's call to put on the Christian armor is *a call to be prepared*. Be ready! Be armed to meet the enemy! Don't wait until it is too late to be prepared. You don't wait until you are in the air to learn to fly a plane. You don't wait until you are on the sea to learn to sail. You don't wait until you are taking your exam to study. You don't wait until danger comes to pray for the first time. Put on your armor before the battle begins. Be prepared. Be equipped to meet the enemy, for he will come.

Empowered by God

Notice also that *the armor comes from God*. You cannot meet the enemy with your strength alone. "Put on the armor of God," Paul says. To put on this ancient armor a soldier needed help. Someone had to help buckle, lift, and fasten straps. This help comes from God. The Christian receives his armor from God. This equipment makes him wholly and completely prepared to go into battle. He could cry with Paul, "I can do all things through Christ." To be strong is to be made powerful by God. Our strength comes from God who empowers us. Apart from Christ, we can do nothing. Our armor is supplied by him.

The Belt of Truth

Paul, then, begins his list of the pieces of the equipment which the Christian soldier is to wear. He begins with "the belt of truth." "Stand therefore, having girded your loins with truth." Stand is a key word. We are not on a march yet or in an assault, but we are required to dig in our footing to prepare for the battle of one's own soul. This is a call for preparatory action.

A soldier could not fight with a loose flowing robe hanging about him. If he had to fight or run, he had to wrap the garment about his body to get it out of his way. A fisherman often tied his robe around himself, so he could work easier. Simon Peter, the fisherman, once wrote "let your mind be girded." Be prepared — be ready.

The girdle of truth was a reference to the wide leather belt which a soldier wore to support his back in long battles and which was also used to hold his knife, club, or small shield. For the Christian, this supportive belt was composed of truth. What is truth? This is a question which philosophers like Aristotle, Socrates, Plato, and others have asked through the ages. The Christian answer to that question responds not with ideas but with a person. Jesus is the truth. "I am the way, the truth and the life," said Christ. Truth is personalized in this man. He is truth, the way of truth, and the way to truth. We experience truth as we gird ourselves in him and the truth of his person. We know truth in submission to the Lord of truth.

It is hard sometimes to find a truthful person, isn't it? Maxwell Anderson in the play <u>Winterset</u> speaks about a person of truth. Mio asks:

> Will you tell me how a man's
> to live, and face his life, if he can't believe
> that truth's like a fire,
> and will burn through and be seen
> though it takes all the years there are?
> While I stand up and have breath in my lungs
> I shall be one flame of that fire;
> It's all the life I have.[27]

We need more persons who will be flames for truth, who will stand up and be one more voice, sometimes the only voice, for <u>truth in one's</u> home, church, community, city, nation, and the

---

27 Maxwell Anderson, *Winterset*, Act II.

world. From Christ, the source of truth, we draw strength to live and speak as we are girded with the truth of his presence.

THE BREASTPLATE OF RIGHTEOUSNESS

Next Paul urges us to "put on the breastplate of righteousness." For a Roman soldier, the breastplate protected the vital organs such as his heart, lungs, and throat. The uprightness of character is what protects the vital organs of a Christian. The moral integrity of a Christian is evidenced in the high standards by which he or she lives. Our world needs more Christians whose inner strength of character enables them to withstand the conflicts around them.

The beautiful little ermine, whose fur is brown in the summer and white in the winter is a fairly easy animal to capture. Hunters have learned to chase it toward mud pits because it will yield its life rather than soil its beautiful coat.

Christian righteousness should be that strong. What a difference Christians would make in the world if they lived always striving to avoid the destructive forces of evil. "Let your light so shine," Jesus said, "that they may see your good works that your heavenly Father might be glorified." In the battle for personal and social justice, the Christian will wage his battle on the front of the battle lines of life. Never forget that the breastplate of righteousness is "put on" by faith. Righteousness is God's gift to us through his forgiveness. We put it on like a robe and wear it to protect us in the world.

Remember that you cannot lay aside the armor of God. The Christian must wear it all the time in the war against sin. The breastplate of righteousness is a piece of spiritual equipment which the Christian wears to protect himself or herself against evil. If one does not fill his life with good, then evil will find lodging within. The battle continues. You might have a beautiful vegetable garden now, but, if you do not weed it tomorrow, it will soon be overcome again with weeds. Battling the weeds is a continuous warfare that is always waged. So, the battle against evil is a constant one. The breastplate of righteousness is our assurance of continuing to battle evil in the world.

SHOD WITH THE GOSPEL OF PEACE

Our feet are to be shod with the preparation of the gospel of peace. Every soldier needs good boots if he is to fight. This hobnailed shoe enabled the soldier to stand on slippery ground and fight his enemy hand-to-hand. The Christian likewise needs a firm foothold so he or she is steadfast and unmovable in the conflicts of life. Our Christian shoes prepare us to be ready for all our difficulties and problems with evil. We can then hold our own against evil.

The readiness we have comes from the gospel of peace which fortifies us. We have peace within, peace with others, and peace with God. We now wage peace, so others can share in the joy we have experienced. But is it peace we bring in our war with evil? We seek to overcome evil with good.

Several years ago, I saw the movie *Pale Rider* starring Clint Eastwood who played a gun fighter called Preacher. It was a good western but was certainly not a religious movie. The solution to the problem of evil was to destroy the enemy. This preacher met hostility with quiet hostility of his own. Vengeance and force won the day. But this is not the Christian answer. The Christian answer is the way of peace. The Christian tries to convert his or her enemy not kill him. Let our feet be shod with peace.

THE SHIELD OF FAITH

Above all, take the shield of faith. In addition to the other pieces of equipment, take the large shield — the one as big as a door — and keep behind it for protection. This rectangular shaped shield covered with several layers of bronze and ox-hide protected the soldier from the fiery darts of the enemy. Our faith is described like a door in the book of Revelation where Jesus said, "Behold I stand at the door and knock and if anyone opens to me I will come in and sup with him." By faith we open the door of our lives to him, and by faith he protects us from the fiery darts of evil.

We are familiar with fiery darts of all kind, are we not? Some are set on fire and hurled at us by gossip, lust, sexual passion, fears, and hatreds. These darts of temptation come without warning and when we least expect them. We need the shield of faith to protect us. Our faith gives us the shield to quench the darts of temptation and fear.

The psalmist declared that God is our sun and shield (Psalm 84:11). Our faith is an acknowledgment that God is really the shield that protects us. It is not we but God who is the source of our strength. He fortifies us and surrounds us with his care. But we must accept his grace as we "take the shield." We have to respond. We must grasp the shield. That is our act of trust. Our shield of faith then goes before us to sustain us — even God himself — our sun and shield.

During the London blitz in the Second World War, a father was seeking to find shelter for his son and himself. He finally found a bomb shelter in the ground and jumped into it. He told his son to jump into the hole after him, but his son was afraid. It was dark, and he could not see his father. His father yelled up to him: "Jump, son. I will catch you. I will not drop you."

Sometimes for us we must make that leap of faith into the darkness of the unknown. We must do it with the assurance of faith that God is there to grasp us and keep us from falling. Faith is the shield that enables us to take that leap into the dark places of life.

THE HELMET OF SALVATION

Take the helmet of salvation. An attendant usually gave a soldier his helmet. He received it from another to put on. We have to receive salvation. It comes to us as God's gift. We receive it from God's hand as his free gift to us.

I think it is interesting that Paul calls it the helmet of salvation. Salvation is often associated with the heart, but here he speaks of protecting the head as the place of salvation. All our mental awareness is involved in the process of salvation. We are to love God with our mind as well as our heart; it requires our total being — a full commitment. Thinking through our faith is a part of being Christian. As long as we have on the helmet, our head is protected. Our enemy may cut off the plumb or dent the helmet, but we are protected nevertheless. Salvation is a continuing process. We have been saved; we are being saved, and we will be saved.

THE SWORD OF THE SPIRIT

Finally, he declares "take the sword of the spirit which is the word of God." This is the only offensive weapon which Paul mentions. All the rest are weapons of defense. The "word of God" is not identified with the Bible, but it involves more. Literally the word means "the thing said."

Throughout the Old Testament it is clear that no prophet or leader of Israel ever spoke for God without a powerful sense of the word of the Lord coming to him. In many ways and places the Old Testament declares that "the word of the Lord came unto" Abram (Genesis 15:1), Ezekiel (Ezekiel 1:3), Micah (Micah 1:1), Isaiah (Isaiah 6), Jeremiah (Jeremiah 1:4, 13; 2:1; 7:1), Hosea (Hosea 1:1) and others. In the Old Testament the phrase "the word of Yahweh" occurs over four hundred times and is the most common way in the Old Testament to describe God's revelation. The meaning of the phrase is not limited merely to words. Greek thought made a distinction between the word and the deed, between speech and action, but this is not true of the Hebrew concept. *Dabar* in Hebrew may be translated as an action or event.

A word can bring about an action or deed. God's word may be "eventful" because his fiat and his effective action are one. This is seen in the creation story in Genesis One where God speaks, and events become a reality. "And God said, 'Let there be light, and there was light'" (Genesis 1:3). God's word was proclaimed, and words became events. God spoke, and something happened.

The Hebrew concept for the word prepared the way for the New Testament declaration that "the Word became flesh." "The Word" of God is not limited to words, or utterances, but is declared, by the Gospel of John, to be Event in the flesh and life of Jesus Christ. Words ring with reminders of Genesis 1:1, when he states: "In the beginning was the Word" (John 1:1). "And the Word became flesh and dwelt among us" (1:14) or to use J, B. Phillips' translation, God "expressed himself." The incarnation became the fullest articulation, disclosure, or utterance possible to unveil the presence of God in a personal and historical way. The New Testament witness, then, was to bear testimony to what the disciples had seen and experienced in the ***Logos,*** God's communication of himself through Jesus Christ. And so, the witness is carried forward by us. The Bible may truly be a part of God's word to us, but his unique word has come in Jesus Christ — the Word.

The sword of the spirit is the sustaining presence of God in our lives. It comes through the Scriptures to us. But it may come through words of hope, encouragement, challenge, judgment, condemnation, witness, appreciation, teaching or preaching of others. The word may come loudly or quietly, quickly or over a long time. But it guides, directs, and inspires us.

Looking through some recent church hymnals, I noticed that most of them no longer carried the hymn, "Onward Christian Soldiers." Is that because of the music being "outdated"? Or because the military image seems remote. Or because so many church members believe they do not belong to the Christian "army". Jesus has challenged his followers to take up our cross and follow him. Most of us may still be in the crowd following Jesus, but not a part of his "regiment." Jesus is calling each of us to follow him. Let's make a commitment to be his disciple and an apostle — one sent in service. So, receive this armor of the Christian soldier now. Be equipped to confront the forces of evil. Prepare to live under its protection. Wear the belt of truth, the breastplate of righteousness, the shoes of readiness, the shield of faith, the helmet of salvation, and the sword of God's word. We cannot lay the armor aside. We bear it for life in our battle against evil.

Several years ago, in a church Christmas play, instead of a doll for baby Jesus, the director had placed a light in the manger. In the middle of the drama, someone accidently turned off the light for the baby Jesus. A little boy yelled, "Hey, you shut off Jesus!" Too many of us have shut off Jesus. Let's turn him back on. Put on the whole armor of God. We are engaged in a battle against evil. Rise up. Let Christ's army be on the move. Like a mighty army moves the church of God. Let it be! Let it be!

14

My Dream For The Church: A Summary

It was a hot August Sunday like many that we have had recently. But it was pre-air-conditioned days. The small crowd gathered in the stuffy, unbelievably warm church. The people gathered without much expectation, because they had been there before. They had heard this preacher and knew what he would say. The choir was pathetically small, dull, and off-key. The congregation sat behind their funeral fans as they looked up at the pulpit without any real expectancy. And their expectations were met as usual with a poorly prepared sermon.

After the service was over, Brother Robin stood at the door greeting the people as they passed by him. The people made such incisive observations as: "Hot day, ain't it, preacher?" "Yeah." "We need rain." "Yes, it would be nice if we got rain," the preacher responded. Suddenly Brother Robin became uncomfortable as he noticed a stranger coming through the line of greeters. He extended his hand to the stranger and said, "Robin is my name." The stranger responded, "Yes, I know." "And yours?" the preacher asked. "Oh, I'm just a watchman," the stranger replied, "A watchman?" "Yes, just a watchman," the stranger said. Then the preacher said to him, "Well, come again." But the watchman made a disarming observation which stuck in the minister's mind when he asked, "Why?"

I have never forgotten that story which I read several years ago. Every preacher, every church member should hear that story ringing in his or her ears. The question should linger: "Why should anyone who is not related to the church ever want to come back again?" All that I have been writing about in this book seeks to address that question and the challenge we have as Christians to reach out to others with the Gospel.

Genesis Chapter 37 records the story where Joseph's brothers looked up from where they were keeping sheep and saw Joseph coming toward them, and they exclaimed: "Behold the dreamer comes. Let us slay him and see what happens to his dreams." Joseph had made his bothers uncomfortable with his dreams to the point they wanted to kill him. I want to confess that I am a dreamer. But I hope that you will not be like Joseph's brothers and choose to use their reaction to deal with the dreamer. The brothers didn't kill Joseph, but instead they threw him in a pit, and then later sold him into slavery. We can find different forms of "slavery," even within the church from those who choose to reject those who dream that the church might be different than the form or organization it presently is.

The Scriptures often depict that those who are touched by God are dreamers. The prophet Joel affirms that one day young men and women-- notice he says women too-- will prophesy and see visions (Joel 2:28). The young church, according to the Book of Acts (Acts 2:14-18), came into existence out of the vision and dreams of the disciples of Jesus as they saw God at work in the world. I am convinced that nothing, absolutely nothing worthwhile has ever been accomplished without dreaming. First there is a dream, then the painting. There is a dream, then there is music. There is a dream, then there is a bridge. There is a dream, and then there is the automobile. There is a dream, and then men and women go exploring across continents, seas, and into outer space. There is first a dream, and then there is a building. The dream inspires persons to move forward as God works within the hearts and minds of individuals.

MY DREAM FOR THE CHURCH

In this chapter, I want to draw together in a summary fashion the basic threads set forth in the other chapters. I want to enu-

The Rebirth of the Church

merate the dream I have for the Church — the local and universal Church. Here briefly is my dream for the Church.

NOT AFRAID OF CHANGE

First, I dream that our church will be unafraid of change. Now I say this because that has not been traditionally true for the Church, not just for the local church but the Church universal. The Church has often set rigid patterns for its traditions and creeds, The Church has often been told to "toe the line." The Church has built its theological fences with the Apostle's Creed, the Nicene Creed, and the Chalcedonian Creed, and others. Within our own Baptist traditions, the London Confession, the Philadelphia Confession, and the Baptist Faith and Message have established our "limits." We constantly want to creedalize our religion. We are really fearful of change. If one differs with or challenges one of our church's basis doctrines, that person is called a heretic.

I believe, if the church truly follows our Lord, it will be unafraid of change. Jesus continually was confronted by the scribes and Pharisees as he challenged their tradition and narrow rigidity about religion. "I have come that you might have life and have it abundantly," Jesus declared. "It has been said unto you, but now I say to you." Jesus came to give a new birth, a new song, a new commandment, and a new covenant. He cut through the religious rigidity of his day to bring new and fresh insight into God's love and way. Jesus challenges his followers to move into the future to follow God no matter where he might lead and not to be anchored to the past.

I mentioned before that several years ago, our church bulletin cover in one of my churches carried some startling lines from a *Home Mission* magazine article which read: "The Seven Last Words of the Church: We Never Did It That Way Before!" The seven last words of the church, revealed in this quote, depict the church with its heels dug in, disclosed in an organization frightened of the future, and unwilling to move into unchartered waters. But

I am convinced that God wants us to sail into the oceans of new opportunities far from the shore. Instead of hugging traditionalism and formalism that anchor us to the past, Christ challenges us to be willing to sail on the edge of heresy to follow our Lord into new insights and deeper truths.

The Priesthood of Believers

Secondly, I dream that the priesthood of believers will be a reality in the Church. When this belief is put into practice, the Church will know that ministry is not just for professional holy persons but the responsibility of all Christians. The primary role of the pastor is to be an equipper. He or she is the one who trains and guides all Christians into their own ministry. I am not the only minister in my church, the professional staff are not the only ministers in their church. There are hundreds and thousands of ministers in church congregations. Every single member is a minister for Jesus Christ. The real ministry of the church will be lay led.

Remember that Jesus himself was a lay person. He called around him twelve persons who were all lay ministers. Stephen and Barnabas were lay ministers. Although Paul was a rabbi, he always earned his own living by making tents. Most of the work of the church is done by lay persons. YOU, as a member of a local church, and not the professionals, are the real ministers.

As I think back over my own life as I grew up in the church. I see many lay persons who had an impact on my life. There was Mr. Martin who taught twelve-year-old-boys. I remember Mrs. Templeton, who directed the youth choir, and Billy Wood, the director of Training Union. In my first church, when I was a college and seminary student, I remember Joe and Christine Good, Bud Lohr, Bob and Madeline Booker and dozens of others who touched the life of a young pastor. In other churches where I have pastored. I see Bea Hulsey, standing six-foot-four, even in his seventies, still teaching a junior class of boys. Many young men today praise Bea Hulsey and the impact he had on their lives. Lionel Pruner, retired manager of the Pet Dairy Company, took cassettes of our worship services into nursing homes. Pam Pace, who week after week added beauty to our worship services as she served as chairman of the flower committee. She saw this as her ministry. Riley Lee, an engineer, served as the choir director of one of the churches where I was pastor.

In another of my congregations, I see Clyde Carroll who began our nursing home ministry that touched fifteen nursing homes and had a hundred people involved in that weekly ministry. I see Katherine Rose who taught preschoolers for fifty years and Lewis Wayne, one of our deacons, who served in so many capacities in our church. I see hundreds of other lay persons who serve faithfully in the name of Christ. The real ministry of Christ cannot be limited to the work of a few professionals. Christ has called all of us into his ministry.

I sat in a conference once and the leader in charge of the group said, "Bill, would you change places with Emily for a moment?" I said, "I am sorry I can't do that." Now I knew what he meant. He wanted me to change seats. I could change seats with her. But I cannot do Emily's work in ministry. She has her gifts, and I have mine. Each of us has his or her gifts. Each of these gifts is important in the work of Christ. Every single person is needed and his or her work is important in the ministry for Christ. The great tragedy is that we often leave the work of the church to the handful of a few professionals, and then wonder why the church limps along. I like the words of Karl Barth, the noted German theologian, who wrote: "There can be no talk of higher and lower order of specific service. There is differentiation of functions, but the preacher cannot really stand any higher than the other elders; nor the bell-ringer any lower than the Professor of Theology. There can be no 'clergy' and no "laity;" no merely 'teaching' and no merely "listening' Church, because there is no member of the Church who is not the whole thing in his own place."[28]

---

28 Karl Barth, article for *The Universal Church of God's Design*, quoted in *The Realm of Redemption* by J. Robert Nelson (Greenwich: The Seabury Press, 1951), 1.

Every single Christian is important in the work of Christ. Every Christian serves as a priest in the Church. The Church of the Savior in Washington, D.C. affirms in their membership statement that the Church of Christ is a ship on which "there are no passengers, all are crew members." Everybody has responsibility in ministry.

A United Church

Thirdly, I dream that the church will be a united Church. To be a united church means that we are tolerant of one another. We are not like the blind men who examined an elephant, and each assumes that he knows what the animal is like because one has the trunk, or the leg, or the ear, or the side. No one person or denomination has all the truth — all the understanding of Christ or his Church. We are diverse in our knowledge of Christ and our gifts, yet we are unified in our love of Christ and commitment to his Church. We acknowledge our many gifts as there are parts of the human body. The body is not merely an ear, or an eye, or a hand. They are all part of the total body. In the body of Christ, each has a part in the unity of the whole. Our diversity in our unity gives us tolerance. The Church can never really be the Church when it is constantly torn with divisiveness, criticisms, and distension. When individuals always feel that if they can't have their way, they will create problems, then these persons do not know real unity. Murmuring and fussing constantly hurts the Church. If a congregation spends all its energy struggling to survive its internal conflicts, it can't really minister. The Church, when it is Church, recognizes diversity and allows for tolerance in its unity. Our larger unity lies in our commitment to serving our Lord.

Recognizes the Importance of Evangelism and Missions

Fourthly, I dream that the Church will be a church that has enthusiasm for evangelism and missions — sharing the gospel of

The Rebirth of the Church 163

Christ with others-- and for growing in a mature faith. Jesus has called us to be witnesses for him. We cannot keep the gospel to ourselves, if we have authentically been touched by Christ. We will want to share the good news of Jesus Christ with others. Healthy evangelism is a vital part of the nature of the true Church. Unfortunately, we have let caricatures and difficulties of evangelism keep us from being real evangelists for Christ.

In one of my churches, we engaged in a special emphasis under the banner of "Good News Celebration" as we attempted to undertake our mandate for evangelism. All of us are called to share the good news of Christ with others. Granted, few congregations have done evangelism as well as they should be doing it. Our congregation was a member of the Long Run Association, made up of about one hundred forty churches, and we were number ten in baptisms. I wish we had been number one. But we were reaching some persons for Christ. The local churches need to have a new enthusiasm for evangelism and a real sense of commitment to reaching persons for Christ. Will the Church be like a "mighty army" as it shares the Gospel with others? I offer some guidelines for our "great commission" in my book, *Authentic Evangelism: Sharing the Good News with Sense and Sensitivity.*[29]

GROWING IN THE FAITH

As the church, we also must do something to help persons grow after they have come to Christ as Lord. If they have become Christians, then we need to help them move deeper into the faith and become more mature Christians. This instruction can happen through Sunday-School, new member classes, worship, special seminars, home Bible studies, and in many other ways. We want to deepen and enrich our faith and never be satisfied with where we are in our knowledge of Christ and his way. Maturity in the faith will prevent the Christian from being disturbed by "every fresh

---

29 William Powell Tuck, *Authentic Evangelism: Sharing the Good News with Sense and Sensitivity* (Valley Forge: Judson Press, 2002).

wind of doctrine' which comes along. As we grow in our faith, hopefully this will enable us to be more open to differences in our doctrines and worship practices and respect those who have beliefs or practices different from ours.

THE MYSTERY OF WORSHIP

I also dream that the Church will have a deep sense of the mystery of worship. When we read the Scriptures, one discovers that from the beginning to the end of them, the writers always point to the holiness of God and the otherness of man/woman. In Isaiah God is seen by the prophet as high and lifted up. The angels exclaim: "Holy, Holy, Holy." The last book in the Bible, *Revelation*, gives an inscription of the holiness of God. Unfortunately, in our own day one of our modern heresies is the attempt to make worship primarily entertainment. We need to remember that worship is not primarily what we get from it. Worship is what we offer God. Worship is our ascription to God, our confession of sin, our acknowledgment of God's power and presence. Too often we try to put worship on the same level with our civic or social clubs and take our models for worship from television evangelists instead of learning from the biblical witness what worship really is. We need to let it be the place where we affirm the reality of God's presence. Let us come into our church which is designed for high, holy worship and appreciate the sense of beauty that surrounds us. Let us affirm this beauty as ancient Israel did when it constructed their Temple to worship God. Let us be thankful for magnificent places we have to gather for worship and come with thanksgiving on our lips. Let us gather to adore and praise God from the joy of our faith. We have opportunities to worship and praise God in whatever kind of church facility we may have. Let us rejoice and be glad in it.

Let me suggest some simple things which we can do to make our church and worship better. We need to remember to be faithful in our attendance. A life is not really enriched in worship if you are

The Rebirth of the Church

what I call a "drop-in worshipper." We need to be regular in our attendance. Secondly, if we take commitments and responsibilities, then be diligent and carry them through. We need to be dependable and bear our load. Thirdly, remember to pray. Pray for those who lead in worship that they might feel our undergirding support. It is difficult to be critical of those for whom we are praying. Prayer binds us together. Fourthly, be an encourager. What every church needs is encouragers like Barnabas in the early church, who was called the Son of Encouragement. Encouragement undergirds a person with love and support.

I like the story which Carlyle Marney told about a young girl who was struggling with chemistry. Her teacher wrote home to her parents because she had gotten a C or D on a chemistry test. "We can't all be chemists," he wrote, "but I wish we could all be Susans." We may not all be great or famous, but we can encourage one another. Affirm the gifts of others and be thankful for them.

SOLID FINANCES

I dream, in the sixth place, that the church will have its finances in good order. This means, of course, that it must learn to control its debt. There is no question that the heavy debt many churches have because of building debt has weighed them down and prevented them from doing some of the things they may have wanted to do in ministry. But I dream that when churches get their debt for their buildings under control that the churches will have a great mission consciousness. I dream that churches will give at least one-third of their budget for causes beyond themselves. I dream they will be concerned with ministering wherever there is need. I dream that churches will not spend most of its money on ourselves, but we will reach out to minister to the world in the name of Christ. Some suggestions to help in this area are found in my book, *The Forgotten Beatitude: Worshiping through Stewardship*.[30]

---

30 William Powell Tuck, *The Forgotten Beatitude: Worshiping through Stewardship* (Gonzales, FL: Energion Publications, 2016).

A Servant Church

I also dream, in the seventh place, that we will be a servant church. I dream that our people will not be concerned so much for what they can get from the church, but what they can do to serve Christ through his church. I dream that the church buildings will continue to be used seven days a week. In several of the churches I served as pastor, we had a lot of activity in the buildings all the time. We could point to the varieties of ministries — a Job Club, an Alzheimer's Day Care, Kindergarten, Nursery, Mother's Day Out, programs for the divorced, widowed, the Wayne E. Oates Pastoral Counseling Center, a Hispanic Ministry, and a HUGG program that reached out to those who were shut in. We had a nursing home ministry, and we had ministries, programs, and activities of all kinds that went on in the church seven days a week. I hope that these kinds of ministries will increase and multiply as all the churches become more deeply aware of our Lord's call to serve and not to be served. We will be most like our Lord when we serve as he gave his life in service.

A Prophetic Church

I dream, in the eighth place, that we will also be a prophetic church. I hope the church will always be willing to challenge evil and speak out against it. I pray that we will not be content to conform to society, but we will raise our voice and speak out against social evil — racism, bigotry, sexism, war, poverty, pollution, drugs — and whatever other problems are in our society. I pray that the church will always be the voice to challenge prejudice, traditions, customs, mores, materialistic values, the playboy style of living, apathy, and ingratitude. The true Church of Jesus Christ will always be challenging us to be more than we are.

The Rebirth of the Church

DOORS OPEN TO ALL

I dream that the church will have doors open to person of all races, colors, ages, sexes with the love and grace of Christ. I dream the church will build bridges to overcome prejudice and bigotry and not erect walls to divide us from one another. I dream the church will respect and minister to all persons—believers or non-believers, assured or inquiring, doubting or trusting, straight or gay, loved or loveless, sick or well, strong or weak—all! I dream, like our Lord, the Church will reach out to the needy, blind, cripple, sick, rejected, unloved, dying—all who have needs.

A JOYFUL CHURCH

I dream that the Church will have a sense of joy to permeate our whole family of believers. Having been touched by the power of God's grace and mercy and having experienced the inner joy of our faith, we will want to share this joy with one another and those outside the faith. I pray that our church's worship will be filled with a vibrant sense of praise and joy as we reflect on what God has done in our lives. I pray that the relationships of church members with one another will overflow from this same inner joy. One of the members of one of my congregations shared with me a prayer that she heard a deacon pray in another church. "Lord," he prayed. "I pray that other people will come to know you through the winsome joy that is within our lives." What a marvelous prayer. I pray that other people will come to know Christ because of the joy in our lives.

A PILGRIM PEOPLE

Finally, I dream that the church will remember that we are a pilgrim people, that we will never arrive in the ministry of Christ. No matter where we are in our pilgrimage of faith, we are always in route. We are still growing, constantly seeking always to understand new ways and new possibilities of serving and ministering in

Christ's name. No one can ever say that he or she has a final handle on truth. We continuously await new truth and new insights from God. I offer some further suggestions about the ministry of the church in my book, *The Church in Today's World*.[31]

How can we bring a dream like this about? First, we must share in this dream. All of us have to dream, too. Secondly, we must believe in the dream and be willing to be involved to see it happen. Thirdly, we have to be willing to sacrifice. We need to sacrifice time, energy, and money, if this dream is to be a reality. ALL of us must be sacrificial in our giving of money, time, and energy, Then, fourthly, we need to realize that some of this dream is already a reality in a modest dimension. Let us rejoice in the reality which we already have and move forward to serve Christ better.

Several years ago, a congregation dreamed a dream about a new place of worship, and they began the construction of their church building. Finally, they completed their building. They had a magnificent structure. The congregation invited one of the leading denominational speakers, and he delivered a stem-winding sermon. After they had finished the service and the preacher was getting ready to say the benediction, suddenly a giant hand appeared and wrote across the front of the church in letters ten feet high: "NOW BUILD ME A CHURCH!"

The church can never be content with magnificent buildings. They do help us to worship. But the building is not the church. After a congregation has a building, it must labor to be the Church that Christ founded. God grant that our dream for the authentic Church will become a reality.

---

31 William Powell Tuck, *The Church in Today's World* (Cleveland, TN: Parson's Porch Books, 2011).

Order from https://energiondirect.com

ALSO FROM ENERGION PUBLICATIONS

by William Powell Tuck

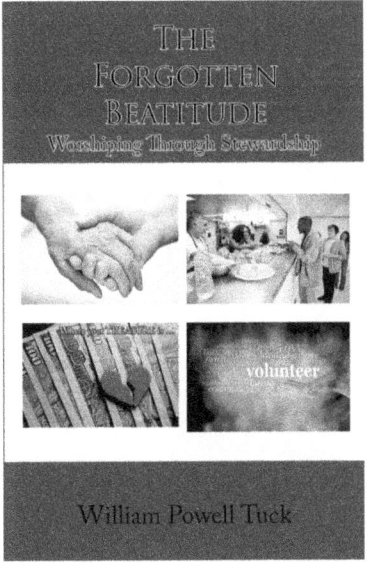

This is certainly a needed response to perhaps the most challenging of topics!

Bo Prosser, Ed. D.
Coordinator of Organizational Relationships, Cooperative Baptist Fellowship
Decatur, GA

Don't let the title fool you … fortunate for us, the questions are deep, the language is clear, and the answers are both deeply profound and simple. This book is for all of us.

Dr. Linda McKinnish Bridges, President, Baptist Theological Seminary at Richmond, Virginia

www.ingramcontent.com/pod-product-compliance
Lightning Source LLC
Chambersburg PA
CBHW031955080426
42735CB00007B/406